The Kenya We Deserve: Building a Nation of Integrity, Innovation, and Unity

Justus Mogaka

WHAT'S INSIDE – KENYA'S ROADMAP TO SUCCESS

KENYA: THE ULTIMATE HERO MOVIE – AND YOU'RE THE MAIN CHARACTER ... 33

INTRODUCTION: THE PATH TO A NEW KENYA ... 36

THE "SPECIAL" NATURE OF OUR CHALLENGES ... 37
CORRUPTION: THE GIFT THAT KEEPS ON TAKING ... 37
TRAFFIC AND MATATUS: A NATIONAL SPORT ... 39
THE POWER OF CULTURAL TRANSFORMATION ... 40
ACCOUNTABILITY: NOT JUST FOR OTHER PEOPLE ... 41
A VISION FOR THE FUTURE: WELCOME TO "FUNCTIONAL KENYA" ... 43
POLITICAL MATURITY: FEWER EMPTY PROMISES, MORE ACTION ... 44
SERVICE DELIVERY: EXCELLENCE WITHOUT THE BRIBE ... 44
SO, HOW DO WE GET THERE? ... 45
THE ROAD AHEAD ... 46

INTEGRITY BEGINS WITH US – COMBATING CORRUPTION FROM THE GROUND UP ... 48

UNDERSTANDING THE ROOTS OF CORRUPTION ... 48
PROMOTING ACCOUNTABILITY IN EVERYDAY LIFE ... 50
HOW CITIZENS CAN HOLD LEADERS ACCOUNTABLE ... 52
CASE STUDIES OF COUNTRIES THAT HAVE SUCCESSFULLY REDUCED CORRUPTION ... 55
CONCLUSION: INTEGRITY STARTS WITH YOU! ... 57

<u>PUBLIC SERVICE FOR THE PEOPLE – RECLAIMING THE HEART OF GOVERNANCE</u> **<u>59</u>**

ENCOURAGING YOUTH TO SEE LEADERSHIP AS A PATH TO NATIONAL TRANSFORMATION 65
BUILDING SYSTEMS THAT REWARD MERIT, NOT CONNECTIONS 67

<u>LEADERSHIP FOR THE FUTURE – NURTURING THE NEXT GENERATION OF KENYAN LEADERS</u> **<u>71</u>**

SOCIAL JUSTICE, HUMAN RIGHTS, AND GOVERNANCE 73
BONIFACE MWANGI – ACTIVISM AGAINST CORRUPTION, HUMAN RIGHTS ABUSES 74
ERIC OMONDI – YOUTH ADVOCACY, UNEMPLOYMENT, AND GOVERNANCE 74
OKIYA OMTATAH – HUMAN RIGHTS, LEGAL REFORMS, ANTI-CORRUPTION 75
JOHN GITHONGO – ANTI-CORRUPTION, TRANSPARENCY IN GOVERNANCE 76
JEROTICH SEII – GOVERNANCE REFORMS, ANTI-BBI MOVEMENT 76
MUTEMI KIAMA – DIGITAL ACTIVISM, TRANSPARENCY IN GOVERNANCE 77
IRUNGU HOUGHTON – HUMAN RIGHTS ADVOCACY, GOVERNANCE REFORMS 77
WANJERI NDERU – ACCOUNTABILITY, GENDER-BASED VIOLENCE, POLICE BRUTALITY 78
MUTHONI WANYEKI – FEMINISM, WOMEN'S RIGHTS, DEMOCRACY ADVOCACY 79
GACHEKE GACHIHI – SOCIAL JUSTICE AND RIGHTS FOR INFORMAL SETTLEMENT DWELLERS 79
AL-AMIN KIMATHI – HUMAN RIGHTS ADVOCACY FOR TERROR SUSPECTS 80
LYNN NGUGI – GENDER ISSUES, SOCIAL JUSTICE STORYTELLING 80
RUTH MUMBI – WOMEN'S RIGHTS, URBAN POOR ADVOCACY 81

JEREMIAH MATAGARO – YOUTH ADVOCACY, ENVIRONMENTAL JUSTICE 81
ENVIRONMENTAL AND SUSTAINABLE DEVELOPMENT **82**
WANGARI MAATHAI – ENVIRONMENTAL CONSERVATION, REFORESTATION 82
PHYLLIS OMIDO – ENVIRONMENTAL JUSTICE, POLLUTION CONTROL 83
FATUMA ABDULKADIR ADAN – PEACE ADVOCACY THROUGH SPORTS AND ENVIRONMENTAL JUSTICE 84
LORNA RUTTO – ECO-FRIENDLY PRODUCTS, PLASTIC RECYCLING 84
TONY NYAGAH – SOLAR ENERGY, SUSTAINABLE ENERGY SOLUTIONS 85
DAVID KURIA – ECO-FRIENDLY SANITATION SOLUTIONS 85
EVANS WADONGO – SOLAR ENERGY PRODUCTS FOR RURAL AREAS 86
MATTHEW RUTO – WASTE MANAGEMENT AND RECYCLING 86

TRUSHNA BUDDHDEV-PATEL – HANDCRAFTED FOOTWEAR PROMOTING SUSTAINABLE FASHION 87
PETER NJONJO – FOOD DISTRIBUTION AND SUSTAINABLE FARMING (TWIGA FOODS) 87
CATHERINE MAHUGU – EMPOWERING ARTISANS THROUGH ECO-FRIENDLY ONLINE MARKETPLACE (SOKO) 88
KENYATTA KANYEKI – SOLAR-POWERED SOLUTIONS FOR RURAL COMMUNITIES 89
TECHNOLOGY AND INNOVATION **89**
JULIANA ROTICH – USHAHIDI PLATFORM, TECH FOR CRISIS MAPPING 90
KEN NJOROGE – MOBILE BANKING AND FINTECH SOLUTIONS (CELLULANT) 90
MARK KAIGWA – DIGITAL MARKETING AND STORYTELLING (NENDO) 91
BRIAN GITTA – NON-INVASIVE MALARIA TESTING (MATIBABU) 91
CYNTHIA WANDIA – DIGITAL BANKING SOLUTIONS (KWARA) 92
EUNICE NJERI – ED-TECH SOLUTIONS (ZYDII) 92

Jihan Abass – Digital-Only Insurance (Griffin Insurance) 93

Valentine Njoroge – Communications Tech (Africa's Talking) 93

Ibrahim Gachanja – Ed-Tech and Productivity Platform (AirKlip) 94

Nekesa Were – Tech Incubation and Innovation Hub (iHub) 95

Anthony Mutua – Renewable Energy Inventions 95

David Ndung'u – Solar Energy Products (M-Kopa Solar) 96

Lavender Ochieng – Youth Development and Mentorship (Ongoza) 96

Leshan Juma – Solar-Powered Off-Grid Energy Solutions (Mbegu Solar) 97

Healthcare **97**

Dr. Maxwell Okoth – Affordable Healthcare (Ruai Family Hospital) 98

Wawira Njiru – Nutrition and Health for School Children (Food for Education) 98

Brian Gitta – Health Tech for Malaria Testing (Matibabu) 99

Nelly Tuikong – Locally Made Beauty Products for African Skin (Pauline Cosmetics) 99

Sheila Waruguru – Empowering Women in Healthcare (Nailab Garments) 100

Peter Njonjo – Food Security and Distribution (Twiga Foods) 100

Ken Njoroge – Financial Solutions for Health and Banking (Cellulant) 101

Youth Empowerment and Education **101**

Amos Mwago – Youth Advocacy, Education, and Entrepreneurship 102

Eunice Njeri – Skills Development Through Online Learning Platforms (Zydii) 102

Elizabeth Gikebe – Agricultural Entrepreneurship and Food Security (Mhogo Foods) 103

Sheilah Birgen – Innovators Mentorship (The Innovators Society) 103

JOEL MACHARIA – FINANCIAL EDUCATION PLATFORM (ABACUS) 104
LYNN NGUGI – SOCIAL JUSTICE STORYTELLING AND YOUTH EMPOWERMENT 104
NEKESA WERE – INCUBATION FOR YOUNG TECH INNOVATORS (IHUB) 105
EUNICE NJERI – ONLINE EDUCATION PLATFORM (ZYDII) 105
SOPHIE GICHUGU – EDUCATION INNOVATION AND TECHNOLOGY INTEGRATION (MOUNT KENYA ACADEMY) 106
FAITH RONO – AGRICULTURAL INNOVATIONS TO EMPOWER SMALLHOLDER FARMERS (AFRIGREEN VENTURES) 106
ENTREPRENEURSHIP AND BUSINESS DEVELOPMENT **107**
ERIC KINOTI – MANUFACTURING (SHADE SYSTEMS EA) 107
TABITHA KARANJA – BEVERAGE INDUSTRY (KEROCHE BREWERIES) 107
NJERI RIONGE – AFFORDABLE INTERNET SERVICES (WANANCHI ONLINE) 108
JOEL MACHARIA – INVESTMENT SOLUTIONS (ABACUS) 108
ERIC KINOTI – MANUFACTURING TENTS AND RELATED PRODUCTS (SHADE SYSTEMS EA) 109
EUGENE MBUGUA – MEDIA AND ENTERTAINMENT (YOUNG RICH TELEVISION LTD) 109
BRYAN KARIUKI – PRACTICAL BUSINESS EDUCATION (HUSTLA MBA) 110
NELLY TUIKONG – COSMETICS FOR AFRICAN WOMEN (PAULINE COSMETICS) 110
BRENDA WAIRIMU – FASHION BUSINESS (TAJI CLOTHING) 111
SUSAN WANJIRU – GARMENT MANUFACTURING (NAILAB GARMENTS) 111
JIHAN ABASS – DIGITAL INSURANCE SOLUTIONS (GRIFFIN INSURANCE) 112
FASHION, MEDIA, AND CREATIVE ARTS **112**
CAROLINE MUTOKO – GENDER ADVOCACY AND MEDIA INFLUENCE 113
NDUNGI GITHUKU – FILMMAKING AND CULTURAL STORYTELLING 113
JULIANA ROTICH – TECH AND DIGITAL STORYTELLING 114

Tatiana Karanja – Sustainable Baby Products (Mama Olive)   114

Brenda Wairimu – Fashion Design and Local Production (Taji Clothing)   115

Megan Mukuria – Empowering Young Girls Through Sanitary Products (ZanaAfrica)   115

Dr. Njoki Ngumi – Creative Arts and Media (The Nest Collective)   116

Sheila Waruguru – Fashion for Job Creation (Black & White Denim)   116

Trushna Buddhdev-Patel – Fashion and Craftsmanship (Ikwetta)   117

The Courtroom Chronicles: Where Drama Meets Delays   **121**

The Bizarre Bribery Circus: How Much for Your Freedom?   123

The Power Imbalance: Justice for the Rich, Injustice for the Poor   126

Judiciary Reforms: A Few Steps Forward, and a Few Back   128

The Role of Technology: From File-Fishing to Digital Justice   130

Conclusion: Justice for All—A Work in Progress   132

KEYPOINTS AND SUMMARY   **134**

EMPOWERING CITIZENS: EDUCATION, HEALTH, AND SOCIAL PROGRESS   **142**

Education as a Tool for Social Mobility and National Progress   **145**

Promoting Lifelong Learning and Vocational Skills   **147**

How to Bridge the Gap Between Urban and Rural Education   **149**

Innovative Educational Initiatives to Inspire   **152**

1. The M-Pesa Foundation Academy   152

2. Bridge International Academies   154

3. AkiraChix   155

CONCLUSION: THE FUTURE OF EDUCATION IN KENYA 156

HEALTH IS WEALTH – BUILDING A CULTURE OF HEALTH AND WELLNESS 158

SHIFTING FROM REACTIVE TO PREVENTIVE HEALTHCARE 160

PROMOTING MENTAL HEALTH AWARENESS IN COMMUNITIES 163

THE ROLE OF CLEAN ENVIRONMENTS AND HEALTHY LIVING IN NATIONAL PROSPERITY 165

BUILDING LOCAL HEALTH SYSTEMS THAT DELIVER QUALITY CARE 167

CONCLUSION: HEALTH IS THE REAL WEALTH 169

EMPOWERING WOMEN, EMPOWERING SOCIETY – THE ROLE OF GENDER EQUALITY IN NATIONAL PROGRESS 172

SHIFTING CULTURAL PERCEPTIONS OF GENDER ROLES 174

HOW EMPOWERING WOMEN IMPROVES FAMILY, COMMUNITY, AND NATIONAL OUTCOMES 176

1. FAMILY OUTCOMES: HAPPY WIFE, HAPPY LIFE 177

2. COMMUNITY OUTCOMES: WOMEN AS PILLARS OF SOCIETY 178

3. NATIONAL OUTCOMES: THE ECONOMIC ENGINE OF EQUALITY 179

STORIES OF KENYAN WOMEN BREAKING BARRIERS AND INSPIRING CHANGE 180

1. WANGARI MAATHAI – ENVIRONMENTAL WARRIOR 181

2. TABITHA KARANJA – ENTREPRENEUR EXTRAORDINAIRE 182

3. PHYLLIS OMIDO – THE VOICE OF THE VOICELESS 183

LEGAL AND CULTURAL REFORMS TO PROMOTE GENDER EQUALITY 184

1. LEGAL REFORMS 184

2. CULTURAL REFORMS 185

CONCLUSION: EMPOWERING WOMEN, EMPOWERING SOCIETY 186

TRADITIONAL MEDICINE: A HEALING HERITAGE THAT REFUSES TO GO AWAY 191

THE BEST OF BOTH WORLDS: MERGING TRADITION WITH MODERN MEDICINE 194

HEALTHCARE ON TWO WHEELS: BODA BODA AMBULANCES AND MOBILE CLINICS 197

TELEMEDICINE: THE DOCTOR WILL SEE YOU… VIA ZOOM 199

THE MOBILE HEALTH REVOLUTION: HEALTHCARE IN THE PALM OF YOUR HAND 202

CONCLUSION: THE FUTURE OF HEALTHCARE IN KENYA 204

YOUTH AS THE ENGINE OF CHANGE – EMPOWERING THE NEXT GENERATION 207

THE YOUTHQUAKE: WHEN GENERATION Z MEETS OLD-SCHOOL LEADERSHIP 210

ENTREPRENEURS-IN-CHIEF: HUSTLING, INNOVATING, AND TAKING OVER 212

SOCIAL MEDIA: THE YOUTH'S POLITICAL PLATFORM AND MEME PLAYGROUND 215

EDUCATION AND INNOVATION: UNLOCKING THE NEXT BIG THING 218

THE YOUTH ECONOMY: JOBS, JOBS, AND MORE JOBS (OR LACK THEREOF) 220

THE FUTURE IS YOUTH: LEADING THE CHARGE FOR A BETTER KENYA 222

KEYPOINTS AND SUMMARY 225

ENTREPRENEURS AS GAME CHANGERS – UNLOCKING INNOVATION AND SELF-RELIANCE 230

SHIFTING FROM JOB-SEEKING TO JOB CREATION 232

HOW ENTREPRENEURSHIP CAN DRIVE NATIONAL DEVELOPMENT 235

JOB CREATION: 235

INNOVATION: 235
BOOSTING THE ECONOMY: 236
REDUCING POVERTY: 237
BUILDING A CULTURE OF INNOVATION AND ADAPTABILITY 237
LESSONS FROM SUCCESSFUL KENYAN ENTREPRENEURS 241
THE FUTURE IS BRIGHT FOR KENYAN ENTREPRENEURS 244

TECHNOLOGY AND THE DIGITAL REVOLUTION –
PREPARING KENYA FOR THE FUTURE 247

THE (MIS)ADVENTURES IN DIGITAL LITERACY 249
FROM "PLEASE RESTART" TO "WE CAN CODE THAT" 251
GOVERNANCE IN THE DIGITAL AGE: "EH, SERIKALI YAKO IKO APP?" 253
EDUCATION AND THE DIGITAL CLASSROOM: "SI YOU GOOGLE?" 255
KENYA AS AFRICA'S TECH HUB: "THE SILICON SAVANNAH" 257
THE LAUGHS AHEAD: TECH FAILS AND FUTURE WINS 258

INFRASTRUCTURE FOR GROWTH – CONNECTING
KENYA TO OPPORTUNITIES 260

THE ROAD TO NOWHERE (AND EVERYWHERE) 262
WHEN THE LIGHTS GO OUT (AGAIN): KENYA'S POWER STRUGGLE 265
BROADBAND DREAMS: THE BATTLE FOR INTERNET CONNECTIVITY 267
BUILDING BRIDGES (AND NOT JUST POLITICALLY) 270
THE FUTURE OF KENYA'S INFRASTRUCTURE: IT'S GONNA BE BIG (AND HILARIOUS) 272

AGRICULTURE AS A PILLAR OF ECONOMIC
DEVELOPMENT – FEEDING THE NATION, FEEDING
THE WORLD 274

THE COMEDY OF TRADITIONAL FARMING   276
ENTER THE AGE OF SMART FARMING   278
SUSTAINABLE FARMING: THE ONLY WAY FORWARD   281
AGRIBUSINESS: THE BILLION-SHILLING INDUSTRY NO ONE SAW COMING   283
FEEDING KENYA, FEEDING THE WORLD   285

INNOVATION IN PUBLIC-PRIVATE PARTNERSHIPS – A COLLABORATIVE APPROACH TO DEVELOPMENT   288

PUBLIC MEETS PRIVATE: LIKE TWO RELATIVES AT A FAMILY WEDDING   290
THE ROAD TO INNOVATION: WHERE PPPs PAVE THE WAY (LITERALLY)   293
SERVICE DELIVERY: WHEN PPPs BRING HEALTH, INTERNET, AND WATER   296
THE PPPs OF THE FUTURE: BOLD IDEAS AND EVEN BOLDER STRATEGIES   299
THE CHALLENGES (AND COMEDY) OF PPPs   302
CONCLUSION: THE FUTURE IS BRIGHT (AND HILARIOUS)   304

BUILDING FINANCIAL DISCIPLINE – FROM CONSUMPTION TO SAVINGS AND INVESTMENT   306

SHIFTING FROM A SPENDING CULTURE TO ONE OF SAVING AND INVESTMENT   308
FINANCIAL LITERACY AS A DRIVER OF PERSONAL AND NATIONAL PROSPERITY   310
COMMUNITY SAVINGS GROUPS AND COOPERATIVES AS TOOLS FOR EMPOWERMENT   313
SACCOs: THE BIG LEAGUES OF COOPERATIVE BANKING   315
PRACTICAL TIPS FOR LONG-TERM WEALTH BUILDING   317
CONCLUSION: FROM CONSUMPTION TO WEALTH CREATION   320
KEYPOINTS AND SUMMARY   322

HEALING OUR LAND – SUSTAINABILITY AND ENVIRONMENTAL STEWARDSHIP 328

THE IMPACT OF CLIMATE CHANGE ON KENYA'S DEVELOPMENT 331
SHIFTING TO SUSTAINABLE AGRICULTURAL PRACTICES 333
COMMUNITY-DRIVEN ENVIRONMENTAL PROTECTION INITIATIVES 337
SAVING KENYA, ONE TREE AT A TIME 342

TOURISM AND CONSERVATION – HARNESSING KENYA'S NATURAL BEAUTY FOR ECONOMIC GROWTH 344

THE TOURIST INVASION: WHEN LIONS HAVE PAPARAZZI 347
WHEN CONSERVATION BECOMES A COMEDY OF ERRORS 350
ECO-TOURISM: WHEN TOURISTS BECOME CONSERVATIONISTS (WHETHER THEY LIKE IT OR NOT) 353
THE FUTURE OF CONSERVATION: MORE TECH, LESS DRAMA 356
THE CIRCLE OF LIFE: KEEPING THE BALANCE 357
HOUSING FOR ALL – TACKLING URBANIZATION AND AFFORDABLE HOUSING 359
THE NAIROBI RENT OLYMPICS: MAY THE ODDS BE EVER IN YOUR FAVOR 362
THE KIBERA DILEMMA: INFORMAL SETTLEMENTS AND THE SEARCH FOR DIGNITY 364
AFFORDABLE HOUSING: THE KENYAN DREAM (WITH A SIDE OF MORTGAGE STRESS) 366
THE GREEN BUILDING CRAZE: SUSTAINABLE URBAN PLANNING (WITH A KENYAN TWIST) 368
THE BODA BODA QUESTION: TRANSPORTING PEOPLE AND LIVELIHOODS 371
HOUSING FOR ALL: THE KENYAN DREAM (YES, EVEN FOR YOU) 372
THE URBAN-RURAL DIVIDE: NAIROBI VS. THE VILLAGE (A TALE OF TWO WORLDS) 378

BRIDGING THE GAP: WHEN DEVELOPMENT HEADS TO THE SHAMBA 380

THE TECH REVOLUTION GOES RURAL: WHEN WI-FI MEETS THE VILLAGE GOAT 383

AGRICULTURE: THE BACKBONE OF RURAL DEVELOPMENT 385

THE IMPORTANCE OF EDUCATION: SCHOOLS IN THE VILLAGE, AND THE CASE OF THE MISSING CHALK 387

THE ROAD AHEAD: TOWARD EQUITABLE DEVELOPMENT 389

KEYPOINTS AND SUMMARY 392

A UNIFIED KENYA – OVERCOMING TRIBALISM AND FOSTERING NATIONAL COHESION 397

UNDERSTANDING THE HISTORICAL ROOTS OF TRIBALISM IN KENYA 399

HOW DIVERSITY CAN BE A STRENGTH RATHER THAN A DIVIDING LINE 402

FOSTERING INTER-ETHNIC COLLABORATION IN POLITICS, BUSINESS, AND COMMUNITY 405

THE ROLE OF MEDIA, SCHOOLS, AND LEADERS IN PROMOTING UNITY 408

CONCLUSION: THE KENYA WE DESERVE 410

SPORTS AND CULTURE – UNITING A NATION THROUGH SHARED HERITAGE 412

THE MARATHON OF LIFE: WHY RUNNING IS IN OUR BLOOD (LITERALLY) 415

THE POWER OF CULTURE: MUSIC, DANCE, AND THE KENYAN SOUL 420

CONCLUSION: THE MARATHON CONTINUES, AND THE BEAT GOES ON 424

REVIVING THE SPIRIT OF UBUNTU – STRENGTHENING FAMILY AND COMMUNITY BONDS 426

REDISCOVERING THE ROLE OF FAMILY AND COMMUNITY IN SHAPING CULTURE   428

THE POWER OF MUTUAL AID AND COLLECTIVE RESPONSIBILITY   430

LESSONS FROM KENYA'S PAST ON THE IMPORTANCE OF COMMUNITY UNITY   432

HOW STRONG SOCIAL FABRIC CAN SUPPORT NATIONAL PROGRESS   435

PRACTICAL STEPS TO STRENGTHEN FAMILY AND COMMUNITY BONDS   437

CONCLUSION: UBUNTU FOR A STRONGER KENYA   440

THE ROLE OF RELIGION AND ETHICS – GUIDING MORALITY AND SOCIAL COHESION   442

A NATION OF MANY FAITHS: THE KENYAN RELIGIOUS MELTING POT   444

SUNDAY MORNING MADNESS: WHERE RELIGION MEETS KENYAN HUSTLE   447

ETHICS AND THE MORAL COMPASS: RELIGION AS KENYA'S UNOFFICIAL REGULATOR   449

RELIGIOUS COHESION: WHEN DIFFERENT FAITHS SHARE THE SAME TABLE   452

RELIGION AND POLITICS: WHEN PREACHERS AND POLITICIANS COLLIDE   455

CONCLUSION: RELIGION AS A GUIDING LIGHT FOR KENYA'S FUTURE   457

KEY POINTS AND SUMMARY   459

DIASPORA CONTRIBUTIONS – TAPPING INTO GLOBAL KENYAN POTENTIAL   463

THE GREAT KENYAN ESCAPE: CHASING DREAMS, DOLLARS, AND WINTER JACKETS   466

REMITTANCES: WHEN A SIMPLE "HUSTLE" BECOMES A LIFELINE   468

KNOWLEDGE TRANSFER: BRINGING THE WORLD TO KENYA, ONE BRAIN AT A TIME   471

GLOBAL NETWORKS: THE DIASPORA'S SECRET SUPERPOWER   474

THE DIASPORA'S COMIC RELIEF: NAVIGATING THE DOUBLE LIFE   476

CONCLUSION: FROM AFAR, WITH LOVE   478

REGIONAL INTEGRATION – KENYA'S ROLE IN EAST AFRICAN AND CONTINENTAL GROWTH   480

THE EAST AFRICAN COMMUNITY (EAC): IT'S LIKE A SIBLING RIVALRY… BUT WITH BORDERS   483

THE AFRICAN UNION (AU): A CONTINENTAL FAMILY GATHERING (WITH A LOT OF SPEECHES)   486

THE AFRICAN CONTINENTAL FREE TRADE AREA (AfCFTA): FREE TRADE, FREE HEADACHES?   489

KENYA AS THE DIPLOMATIC POWERHOUSE: PEACEKEEPING, MEDIATION, AND CONFLICT RESOLUTION   492

THE HILARIOUS REALITY OF REGIONAL POLITICS: BORDER DISPUTES AND "FRIENDLY" RIVALRIES   493

CONCLUSION: THE FUTURE OF REGIONAL INTEGRATION – KENYA'S ROLE IN LEADING THE WAY   495

IMMIGRATION AND BORDER SECURITY – BALANCING OPENNESS AND NATIONAL SAFETY   498

THE BORDER IS NOT JUST A LINE: KENYA'S UNIQUE GEOGRAPHICAL CHALLENGE   500

REFUGEES AND IMMIGRATION: THE WORLD AT KENYA'S DOORSTEP   502

BORDER SECURITY: BUILDING WALLS, CHASING SMUGGLERS, AND THE CASE OF THE FLOATING FISHERMEN   506

CONCLUSION: THE ART OF BORDER MANAGEMENT, KENYAN STYLE   512

PEACE AND SECURITY – THE FOUNDATION OF NATIONAL STABILITY   514

THE GREAT KENYAN PEACE SUMMIT: WHEN EVERYONE IS A NEGOTIATOR 517
THE POST-ELECTION DRAMA: A NATIONAL TRADITION 519
THE ABSURDITY OF KENYAN SECURITY: MORE COMEDIC THAN YOU'D EXPECT 521
THE ROLE OF THE KENYAN POLICE: PROTECTORS, NEGOTIATORS, AND SOMETIMES, COMEDIANS 524
SUSTAINABLE PEACE: MORE THAN JUST SECURITY 527
CONCLUSION: BUILDING A MORE PEACEFUL, SECURE (AND SOMETIMES HILARIOUS) KENYA 528
KEY POINTS AND SUMMARY 530

THE POWER OF CIVIC ENGAGEMENT – ACTIVE CITIZENSHIP FOR A FUNCTIONAL NATION 534

THE ROLE OF CITIZENS IN HOLDING GOVERNMENT ACCOUNTABLE 536
TRANSPARENCY 539
HOW CIVIC ACTION LEADS TO BETTER PUBLIC SERVICES 542
CASE STUDIES OF GRASSROOTS MOVEMENTS IN KENYA 545
CONCLUSION: ACTIVE CITIZENSHIP FOR A FUNCTIONAL NATION 548

MEDIA AND INFORMATION – SHAPING NATIONAL IDENTITY AND ACCOUNTABILITY 550

THE MEDIA THEN AND NOW: FROM GOVERNMENT BROADCASTS TO #KOT 553
MEDIA AND ACCOUNTABILITY: EXPOSING THE TRUTH, ONE SCANDAL AT A TIME 556
DIGITAL MEDIA: SHAPING PUBLIC DISCOURSE AND DEMOCRACY 561
CONCLUSION: THE MEDIA'S ROLE IN SHAPING A NATION 564

CULTURE OF INNOVATION – FOSTERING CREATIVITY AND PROBLEM-SOLVING 569

Jua Kali Mentality: Innovating Without a User Manual 572
Education: From "Cramming" to "Creating" 574
Innovation in Industry: From Silicon Savannah to Solar-Powered Shambas 577
Government Innovation: Yes, You Read That Right 580
Conclusion: A Nation of Innovators, Dreamers, and Problem-Solvers 584
KEYPOINTS AND SUMMARY 586

CONCLUSION 589

A CALL TO ACTION – TOGETHER, WE CAN BUILD A BETTER KENYA 589

1. Reaffirm the Vision for a New Kenya 590
2. Highlight the Collective Responsibility 592
3. Call for Immediate and Long-Term Actions 594
A Nation Built on Action, Not Just Words 597

Kenya: The Ultimate Hero Movie – And You're the Main Character

Alright folks, let's be real for a second. Kenya is packed with potential that could blow minds, but it also has those moments where you just scratch your head and think, "How did we end up here?" It's like watching a movie you've seen a hundred times, knowing the ending has to change at some point—the hero can't keep losing, right? We deserve better. This book isn't for putting on a shelf and forgetting, it's the blueprint for a future so legendary it could rival a *Nyama Choma* stop over at Kikopei.

Here's the deal—Kenya has the brains, the muscle, and the vibe to go far, but it's the "action" part that seems to be stuck in neutral. When you look at the situation, it's like a buffet of challenges: corruption, tribalism, an economy that's juggling more than a circus, but we also have flashes of brilliance. I mean, we've got people running businesses from handcarts to tech hubs! That's where we come in. If we come together as a team, we can build this thing. We need to have a mindset of integrity and unity, because without those, we're just spinning our wheels in the mud.

And just to be clear—this isn't just the government's job. Nope. It's on all of us. This book is the playbook for how every one of us—yes, you too—can build a country we can all be proud of. Whether you're into tech, farming, or just the chairperson of your neighborhood WhatsApp group, it's time to roll up your sleeves. Let's leave behind the petty politics and plant the seeds for a future that's truly awesome.

So if you're ready, buckle up and join the ride to building the Kenya we all deserve. The time for whining is over—it's time to take action! Let's make this country the ultimate

hero movie, and guess what? You're the main character.
Let's get to work!

•

Introduction: The Path to a New Kenya

Welcome to Kenya, the land of breathtaking landscapes, legendary marathon runners, and matatus that defy the laws of physics and traffic regulations. We are a country of great potential, amazing people, and, let's not forget, a culture of "I will be there in five minutes" that actually means two hours. Kenya is a land of many contrasts. We have some of the most beautiful places on earth, yet at the same time, we are trying to figure out how a pothole can have its own zip code. So buckle up, ladies and gentlemen, as we embark on a journey through the "Path to a New Kenya"—a Kenya that actually works! (Yes, you heard right!)

The "Special" Nature of Our Challenges

Now, let's get this out of the way: Kenya is special. Not in the "we won a prize" kind of way, but in the "we have our own way of doing things" kind of way. We're the people who will build an entire road and forget to add drainage systems. We're the country where you can start your morning by boiling water on a jiko, but by lunchtime, you're in a high-rise office building closing deals with clients across three continents. It's the land of paradoxes, where brilliance meets bewilderment daily. But hey, that's what makes us, well…us!

Corruption: The Gift That Keeps on Taking

Let's start with the elephant in the room: corruption. It's like that annoying relative who never leaves, no matter how hard you try to ignore them. In Kenya, corruption is a full-time job, complete with benefits. But here's the twist— nobody applied for it, yet it's become part of our everyday culture. Whether it's the public servant skimming off project funds or the traffic cop who's ready to "discuss" your speeding ticket, corruption feels as Kenyan as chai and mandazi.

But it doesn't have to be this way. Just imagine a Kenya where bribes are like mullets—outdated, ridiculous, and seen as a bad fashion statement. A Kenya where you can get a birth certificate in a day without having to know your cousin's best friend's neighbor, who knows someone in the Department of Confusing Paperwork. A place where public funds go toward actual projects and not building private mansions with swimming pools bigger than Lake Nakuru. We can dream, right?

Traffic and Matatus: A National Sport

Another hallmark of our uniqueness is the traffic. Nairobi traffic is like a video game, except there are no rules, and everyone else seems to be playing a different game. There's nothing quite like the thrill of a matatu squeezing between two lanes that don't exist, while simultaneously blasting reggae music so loud you forget you were late to work to begin with. Our traffic jams are a symphony of hooting, frustration, and life decisions. At some point, you just give up and buy samosas from the guy weaving through cars.

But what if—stay with me now—we had a functional public transport system? What if we could actually predict when the next bus will arrive without having to consult a diviner? What if road signs weren't just for decoration? The day we figure out traffic will be the day we crack the code to time travel because surely, with our current levels of chaos, anything is possible!

The Power of Cultural Transformation

Now, onto something more serious. Beneath all these quirky issues, there is a deeper problem. It's not just about potholes or matatus playing musical chairs on the highway. It's about culture—our attitudes, our behaviors, and our collective mindset as a nation. We've all grown up hearing the saying "This is Kenya," often used as an excuse when things go wrong. It's become a cultural shrug, a way to dismiss any possibility of change. But what if we flipped that narrative?

Imagine a Kenya where "This is Kenya" means something entirely different. What if it meant efficiency, transparency, and innovation? What if being Kenyan became synonymous with doing things the right way, with integrity and pride? Changing our culture isn't easy, but it's the key to unlocking the true potential of our nation. You can't expect new results with the same old habits. It's time for us to rewrite the script.

Accountability: Not Just for Other People

Let's talk accountability. It sounds boring, I know, but hear me out. Accountability doesn't mean endless meetings where people "promise to form a committee to look into the issue." It means actually doing what you say you will do. Imagine if leaders were as accountable as the guy who delivers your sukuma wiki at the market—on time, every time, and without asking for a "facilitation fee." A cultural shift toward accountability could change everything. Public servants would serve the public, not themselves. Politicians would run campaigns based on actual policies, not who can dish out the most maize flour at a rally.

And, get this—if we start holding ourselves accountable in everyday life, we won't need to rely on leadership alone. What if we all showed up on time? What if we didn't cut corners (both metaphorically and literally, on the road)? What if we stopped waiting for "someone else" to fix things and took responsibility for our own actions? That's how cultural change starts—from the ground up.

A Vision for the Future: Welcome to "Functional Kenya"

Picture this: It's the year 2030. Kenya has become a model for development. Our hospitals are well-equipped, our roads are paved and pothole-free (I know, stay with me here), and public transport runs like clockwork. Government services are digital and efficient—you can renew your driver's license online in minutes. Traffic jams? A thing of the past, thanks to excellent infrastructure and driver discipline (yes, I said discipline). Nairobi is no longer ranked among the most stressful cities in the world but instead boasts clean streets, green spaces, and an efficient transport system. It's a Kenya where "the system is broken" is a phrase you only hear in history books.

Political Maturity: Fewer Empty Promises, More Action

In this future Kenya, politics isn't about tribal lines or who can shout the loudest at rallies. It's about real policies, real solutions. Leaders are chosen based on merit, integrity, and vision—not how well they can stir up emotions with empty promises. Voting becomes a civic duty driven by informed choices, not freebies or tribal affiliations. Politicians actually deliver on their campaign pledges (I know, shocking), and there's a culture of transparency that makes it impossible to loot public coffers without being caught.

Service Delivery: Excellence Without the Bribe

In this new Kenya, public services are a joy to engage with (yes, a joy!). Gone are the days of bribing your way to get a passport, land title, or anything else that should already be your right as a citizen. A bribe? What's that? In fact, future generations of Kenyans will laugh when they hear about the days when you had to "know someone" to get things done. Public offices will be filled with helpful, efficient staff, eager to assist. Can you imagine that?

So, How Do We Get There?

Here's the kicker—it's going to take more than wishful thinking and hopeful speeches. Cultural transformation requires action. It's not about waiting for someone else to start; it's about each of us making the small, necessary changes in our daily lives. It starts with the everyday Kenyan—the mama selling fruit by the road, the matatu driver, the student, the politician. Everyone has a role to play.

Start small: Show up on time. Refuse to pay or accept bribes. Demand accountability from leaders. Vote wisely. Teach children the values of honesty, hard work, and integrity. Encourage innovation and entrepreneurship. Support local businesses. Use your influence, no matter how small, to promote positive change. Before you know it, the culture begins to shift, and with it, the entire nation.

The Road Ahead

The path to a new Kenya is not going to be easy, and it certainly won't happen overnight. But just imagine the possibilities. Kenya has everything it needs to succeed—natural resources, a young and vibrant population, and, most importantly, a resilience that has carried us through decades of adversity. All we need now is to take the next step: changing our culture and attitudes.

It's time to stop shrugging and saying, "This is Kenya" when things go wrong. It's time to start saying, "This is Kenya!" with pride, when things go right. Together, we can reclaim our future, break the chains of corruption, inefficiency, and division, and build the functional, prosperous Kenya we all deserve.
So let's get to work—because this is Kenya, and we can do better!

Integrity Begins with Us – Combating Corruption from the Ground Up

Ladies and gentlemen, buckle up, because we're about to embark on a journey into the heart of corruption—the thing that turns perfectly decent human beings into monsters who can't resist the urge to pocket public funds faster than you can say "budget deficit." It's not just about what happens behind closed doors in dark corridors of power. Oh no, corruption is like that cousin who shows up at your house, eats all your food, and then asks for fare to get home. It's everywhere, and it's time we had a little chat about it.

Understanding the Roots of Corruption

Now, let's take a minute to understand how corruption starts. Picture this: a well-meaning government official (we'll call him Mr. Njoroge) enters his new office on his first day, full of optimism. He's ready to serve his country, to make his people proud. But then it happens. The first bribe lands on his desk like an unwanted fruitcake. It's from a contractor who looks like he just walked out of a movie about dodgy businessmen.

The contractor smiles, slides the money across the table, and says something along the lines of, "You know, just a small token of appreciation for moving my project forward a little quicker." At that moment, Mr. Njoroge has two choices: be a hero and say no, or take the money and suddenly discover that he needs a new car, a trip to Dubai, and maybe even a house on the beach. He hesitates for a second—and bam! Just like that, corruption is born.

But don't be too hard on Mr. Njoroge. Corruption doesn't happen in a vacuum. It grows from societal norms, systemic problems, and sometimes, plain old human greed.

It's not like people wake up one day thinking, "You know what would really improve my day? Embezzling some public funds." No, corruption is nurtured by a culture that rewards shortcuts, a system that punishes honesty, and a public that shrugs its shoulders and says, "Eh, that's just how things are." But it doesn't have to be that way!

Promoting Accountability in Everyday Life

Before we start pointing fingers at the big shots in government, let's have a quick look in the mirror. Yes, you, dear reader. We're all guilty of feeding the corruption beast. Think about the last time you tried to "speed up" the process at a government office by sliding a little something to the clerk. Or maybe you "knew a guy who knows a guy" who could sort out your issue without all the red tape.

Here's the thing: accountability starts with us. Imagine a world where everyone stopped offering bribes. The traffic police officer pulls you over for speeding, and instead of trying to slip them a Ksh 500 note, you say, "Write the ticket, officer. I deserve it." That officer would probably faint on the spot. And when they come to, they might start thinking, "Wait, maybe I should stop expecting bribes if no one's offering them anymore."

It's like breaking up with a toxic habit—painful at first, but eventually, everyone feels a lot better. The mechanic, the shopkeeper, the local official—when they see that you're not trying to buy your way out of everything, they might just start thinking, "Hey, maybe we should try this accountability thing too." Who knows? Maybe even Mr. Njoroge will turn his life around after reading this chapter and return that beach house.

How Citizens Can Hold Leaders Accountable

Now, let's talk about the fun part—how we, the ordinary citizens of this great nation, can actually hold our leaders accountable. First, let's acknowledge that many of our leaders have an uncanny ability to make us forget they work for us. They strut around like they're doing us a favor, wearing sunglasses indoors, and sitting in air-conditioned offices while we're sweating in queues for basic services. But here's the kicker: we're their bosses! They work for us, and it's about time we started acting like it.

Step one: **Demand transparency.** You see, leaders have a special love for secrecy. They'll pass a national budget, and suddenly, there's a line item that says "Miscellaneous Expenditure: Ksh 100 million," and we're all just supposed to shrug and go, "Well, I'm sure that's necessary." No! Ask questions! Go to town hall meetings, attend public forums, send letters, emails, tweets—whatever it takes. If they claim they spent Ksh 5 billion on upgrading a road that still looks like a scene from a post-apocalyptic movie, demand receipts.

Step two: **Use the power of the vote.** Politicians seem to think that election season is like a reality TV show where they make promises, and we cheer them on like it's entertainment. But this is not a season finale of "Nairobi Housewives." If your leader has spent their entire term doing nothing but renovating their mansion, building a personal hospital, and buying fancy cars, don't re-elect them. Don't fall for the handshakes, the gifts, the little "thank you" parcels they give out during campaigns. No amount of free t-shirts and lesos can fix a bad leader.

Step three: **Whistleblowing is not just for referees.** If you see corruption happening, say something! I know, I know—whistleblowers don't exactly get celebrated like Olympic athletes. In fact, they're more likely to get the side-eye from neighbors and relatives who say, "Why did you have to stir up trouble?"

But whistleblowing is the ultimate act of bravery in this fight. You're not just helping clean up the system—you're actively contributing to building a better future for everyone.

Case Studies of Countries That Have Successfully Reduced Corruption

At this point, you're probably thinking, "This all sounds great, but can it really happen?" Well, my friend, the answer is a resounding YES! Other countries have done it, so why can't we?

Let's start with **Singapore**. Once upon a time, Singapore was just another struggling post-colonial nation with corruption oozing out of every government office. But then, along came a guy named Lee Kuan Yew, who had exactly zero tolerance for corruption. He treated corruption like an infectious disease and made sure that anyone caught indulging in it was removed from office faster than you can say "resignation letter." He created a culture of accountability, transparency, and harsh punishment for corrupt officials. And now, Singapore is one of the least corrupt countries in the world. Plus, they have some pretty great infrastructure to show for it!

Next, we have **Rwanda**. Yes, Rwanda—right here in Africa! Rwanda's president, Paul Kagame, made it clear that corruption was not going to be tolerated. His administration implemented strict laws and took a no-nonsense approach to anyone caught in corrupt activities. They even set up anti-corruption courts to ensure that cases are dealt with swiftly. Today, Rwanda stands out as a shining example of an African country that has made tremendous progress in reducing corruption, and they're on a steady path toward development. And yes, their roads are *actually* fixed when the government says they'll be fixed.

Lastly, we have **Georgia**, a country that literally decided it had enough of being a joke in the corruption world. Under President Mikheil Saakashvili, Georgia fired over 30,000 corrupt police officers in one day! One day! They didn't even bother with long investigations and drawn-out court cases. They cleaned house, made government operations more transparent, and completely overhauled their police force. Today, Georgia is a corruption-fighting powerhouse in Eastern Europe.

Conclusion: Integrity Starts with You!

So, where does that leave us, dear reader? Well, if countries like Singapore, Rwanda, and Georgia can rise from the ashes of corruption, so can we. But it starts with us. Corruption is not some big, bad, untouchable monster. It's the little things that we do every day that contribute to the problem—or solve it. So the next time someone tries to "speed up the process" for you or offers you a bribe, be a hero. Say no. Make them faint with shock if you have to.

Integrity begins with us. The leaders will follow once they see that we, the people, have decided that enough is enough. We're the ones who can break this cycle of corruption, but it will take a cultural revolution of accountability, transparency, and collective action. So, let's do this. Let's reclaim our future, one small act of integrity at a time.

And who knows? Maybe one day, we'll be reading about Kenya in the list of countries that successfully beat corruption. Wouldn't that be something?

Public Service for the People – Reclaiming the Heart of Governance

Ladies, gentlemen, and fellow Kenyans, let's talk about a topic that is both serious and hilarious—**public service**. Yes, public service—the noble profession that, at least in theory, is supposed to be about **serving the people**. But in Kenya, public service has sometimes become more about serving... well, yourself. Somewhere along the way, things got a little twisted, and it feels like we're living in a tragicomedy where the people who are supposed to be making our lives easier are often the ones making us question why we ever learned the word "bribe."

But before we dive into the absurdity, let's set the record straight: **public service is supposed to be a sacred calling**. It's about governance that actually works for the people, not against them. It's about leaders who care more about the nation's prosperity than their own. And, most importantly, it's about reclaiming the heart of governance in Kenya—a heart that has, let's be honest, been on life support for a while now.

The True Meaning of Public Service

Once upon a time (before the advent of brown envelopes and mysteriously inflated tenders), **public service** meant working for the greater good. Picture this: a leader who wakes up in the morning, looks at the national flag, and says, "How can I make life better for my fellow Kenyans today?" That's right—it's not about which brand of Range Rover they'll buy or which palatial mansion they'll add to their collection. It's about **serving the public**—you know, the people who voted them in.

Public service is supposed to be the backbone of a well-functioning society. From the person issuing your national

ID to the folks ensuring that our roads don't look like something out of a war zone, every role is crucial. When public service works, the country thrives. Roads get built (and stay built), hospitals are well-stocked, schools function, and water flows from taps like it's supposed to. When it doesn't work, well… you get what we've seen far too often: potholes big enough to swallow matatus, schools without desks, and government offices where the only thing moving faster than a snail is the person running for lunch.

Now, don't get me wrong. Not every public servant is bad. We've got plenty of hardworking Kenyans in government offices doing their best to make a difference. But the truth is, the system has been hijacked by a few bad apples who seem to think that **public service means personal enrichment**. And here's where things get funny (or sad, depending on your perspective). You walk into a government office, and you're more likely to hear "hakuna system" than anything remotely helpful. You need a document processed? Come back tomorrow. You need something approved? "Talk nicely to me." It's like we're all extras in a sitcom that no one signed up to star in.

But here's the kicker: **public service doesn't have to be this way**. We can—and should—reclaim its true meaning. It's about **serving the people with integrity, humility, and dedication**. It's about seeing public office not as a place to make quick cash but as a place to create long-lasting change. After all, true leadership isn't about how much you can take—it's about how much you can give.
Celebrating Selfless Leaders and Ethical Governance

Believe it or not, **ethical governance** and **selfless leadership** are not unicorns. They exist! We just don't talk about them as much because, well, good news doesn't make headlines like scandals do. But today, let's give credit where credit is due and celebrate some of the **selfless leaders** who have quietly, and sometimes loudly, made a difference in Kenya.

First up, let's talk about the late **Wangari Maathai**. Here was a woman who could have easily joined the ranks of corrupt officials, cashed in on her fame, and spent her days lounging on the beaches of Mombasa. But instead, she chose to fight for the environment and for the people. Wangari Maathai didn't just plant trees—she planted the seeds of a movement that transformed the way we think about environmental stewardship. She put her neck on the line (literally) to fight for what she believed in. That, my friends, is **public service at its finest**.

Or how about **John Githongo**, the former Permanent Secretary for Governance and Ethics, who risked his life to blow the whistle on the infamous Anglo Leasing scandal? This man didn't run for the hills when he saw corruption— he stood tall, exposed the rot, and reminded us all that there are still people out there who believe in **doing the right thing**. Sure, he had to flee the country for a bit (okay, more than a bit), but his actions showed that integrity in public service is not an impossibility. It's just a bit rare—like finding a functional traffic light in Nairobi.

These leaders, and many others like them, remind us that **ethical governance is not a pipe dream**. It's real, and it's possible. But it requires courage, conviction, and the willingness to put the country's needs above your own. It's about seeing leadership as a chance to uplift, not exploit.

Encouraging Youth to See Leadership as a Path to National Transformation

Here's where things get interesting. For too long, we've made **leadership** seem like something that's reserved for old men in suits who've been playing the political game since before independence. But here's a radical idea: **youth can, and should, be leaders**. And I'm not just talking about youth rallies or singing "We are the future" at random events. I mean real, substantive leadership where young people are shaping the future of Kenya, not just waiting for their turn.

The truth is, **Kenya's youth** are a force to be reckoned with. We're talking about the most innovative, tech-savvy, ambitious generation this country has ever seen. If anyone's going to solve our problems—whether it's corruption, unemployment, or the national sugar shortage—it's going to be the youth. But we've got to encourage young people to see leadership not as a way to get rich quick, but as a way to **transform the nation**.

We need to stop telling our kids, "Get good grades so you can get a good job." Instead, we should be saying, "Get good grades so you can change the world." Leadership isn't just about holding office—it's about taking responsibility, having a vision, and inspiring others to follow you toward a brighter future. And guess what? You don't need a title to be a leader. You can start in your community, in your school, or even on your social media page (yes, you TikTok influencers—I see you).

Think about it: if young people start seeing leadership as a path to **national transformation**, we'd have a whole generation of **ethical, visionary leaders** who are more interested in solving problems than in signing dodgy tenders. The youth need to know that the power to change Kenya doesn't lie with the "old guard"—it lies with them.

Building Systems That Reward Merit, Not Connections

Now let's address the elephant in the room—**connections**. We all know that in Kenya, it's not always about what you know—it's about who you know. You could be the most qualified person for a job, but if you don't have that all-important "connection" (read: uncle, auntie, or distant cousin who knows someone in power), you might as well kiss your dreams goodbye.

But it doesn't have to be this way.

Meritocracy—the idea that people should be rewarded based on their abilities and achievements, not their family ties—is not just a Western fantasy. It's something we can, and should, strive for in Kenya. Imagine a world where the best and brightest rise to the top, not because they know someone, but because they've earned it. Crazy, right? Building a system that rewards **merit** means doing away with the **nephew-first hiring policy**. It means creating an environment where hard work, innovation, and dedication are what get you ahead—not whose number you have saved on your phone. This goes for public service, business, and pretty much every sector of the economy.

In a merit-based system, we'd have public servants who are actually qualified for their jobs (shocking, I know). We'd have leaders who know what they're doing and who are committed to the common good. And we'd have a country that thrives because the people in charge are the best people for the job—not the ones with the most connections.

To build this kind of system, we need to start by holding ourselves accountable. We need to stop normalizing nepotism and corruption. We need to call out unfair hiring practices when we see them. And most importantly, we need to **demand better** from our leaders. Because at the end of the day, we get the public service we deserve.
Conclusion: Reclaiming the Heart of Governance

So, what's the bottom line? **Public service** is not supposed to be a punchline. It's not supposed to be a place where corruption, inefficiency, and personal gain reign supreme. Public service is supposed to be about **the people**—about making life better for Kenyans from all walks of life. It's time to **reclaim the heart of governance**.

We need to celebrate our **selfless leaders**, encourage our youth to step into leadership roles, and build a system that rewards **merit, not connections**. It won't happen overnight, but it can happen if we all do our part.
And who knows? Maybe one day, we'll wake up in a Kenya where public service is actually about serving the public. Now wouldn't that be something?

Leadership for the Future – Nurturing the Next Generation of Kenyan Leaders

Kenya has long been a land of boldness, resilience, and passion, but nothing embodies this more than the remarkable leaders across various fields who are paving the way for a brighter future. From fighting corruption to environmental conservation, from advocating for youth empowerment to driving technological innovations, these leaders are redefining what it means to lead in Kenya.

But let's be honest: leadership in Kenya has had its ups and downs. We've seen the **power-hungry elites** take the stage, deliver flowery speeches, and vanish when it's time to actually do the work. It's time we shift the narrative from self-serving leadership to **servant leadership**—a leadership that's about uplifting others, fighting for justice, and building a better society. And who's going to lead this charge? The **next generation** of Kenyan leaders, who are already driving change across the nation.

Let's dive into the contributions of these Kenyan trailblazers in social justice, environmental advocacy, technology, healthcare, and more, who are giving us hope that the future is indeed bright.

Social Justice, Human Rights, and Governance

This group of leaders is fighting tirelessly to ensure that human rights, transparency, and justice are at the forefront of Kenyan governance. Their relentless advocacy is shaping the Kenya we want to see—a country where accountability isn't just a buzzword, but a reality.

Boniface Mwangi – Activism Against Corruption, Human Rights Abuses

Boniface Mwangi is the loud, unapologetic voice of **activism against corruption**. He's not one to mince words, whether he's exposing government graft or marching in the streets for human rights. Through art, protests, and sheer willpower, Boniface has become a symbol of the fight against **human rights abuses** in Kenya. His work reminds us that activism isn't a side gig—it's a lifetime commitment to making things right.

Eric Omondi – Youth Advocacy, Unemployment, and Governance

Who said comedy can't change the world? **Eric Omondi**, the hilarious yet outspoken comedian, is proving that laughter can lead to serious conversations about **youth unemployment** and **governance**. He's used his platform to advocate for the youth, challenging leaders to create job opportunities and take youth issues seriously. When Eric speaks, the youth listen—and the government? Well, they'd better start paying attention.

Okiya Omtatah – Human Rights, Legal Reforms, Anti-Corruption

If you ever need someone to take on the government in court, **Okiya Omtatah** is your guy. This relentless human rights defender has filed more lawsuits against corruption than some of us have had cups of chai. Omtatah's work in **legal reforms** and **anti-corruption** has been instrumental in keeping the Kenyan government on its toes, ensuring that the law works for the people—not the powerful.

John Githongo – Anti-Corruption, Transparency in Governance

John Githongo is practically a synonym for **anti-corruption** in Kenya. His whistleblowing on the infamous Anglo Leasing scandal shook the nation and exposed the deep rot within the government. Githongo's fight for **transparency in governance** continues, as he pushes for a future where Kenyan leadership is about accountability, not backroom deals.

Jerotich Seii – Governance Reforms, Anti-BBI Movement

When the government launched the Building Bridges Initiative (BBI), **Jerotich Seii** stood at the forefront of the **anti-BBI movement**, arguing that it wasn't in the best interest of Kenyans. Jerotich fights for **governance reforms** that focus on improving systems and addressing the real issues that Kenyans face, rather than pushing political agendas.

Mutemi Kiama – Digital Activism, Transparency in Governance

In the age of social media, **Mutemi Kiama** is leading the charge in **digital activism**, using platforms like Twitter to call for **transparency in governance**. Kiama isn't afraid to use memes and witty commentary to expose government failures and demand accountability, showing that activism can thrive in the digital era.

Irungu Houghton – Human Rights Advocacy, Governance Reforms

Irungu Houghton is a human rights warrior who focuses on **governance reforms** to ensure that Kenya's government upholds the rights of its citizens. Whether it's pushing for fair elections or advocating for marginalized communities, Houghton's work ensures that human rights remain a priority in Kenya's governance.

Wanjeri Nderu – Accountability, Gender-Based Violence, Police Brutality

Fighting on multiple fronts, **Wanjeri Nderu** is an advocate for **accountability**, especially in the fight against **gender-based violence** and **police brutality**. She's leading the charge in holding law enforcement accountable and ensuring that women's rights are protected. Nderu's activism is a beacon of hope for those who seek justice in a broken system.

Muthoni Wanyeki – Feminism, Women's Rights, Democracy Advocacy

Muthoni Wanyeki is the embodiment of **feminism** in Kenya, tirelessly advocating for **women's rights** and **democracy**. She's fought for the inclusion of women in leadership and governance, ensuring that Kenya's future includes the voices and contributions of women at all levels of society.

Gacheke Gachihi – Social Justice and Rights for Informal Settlement Dwellers

Gacheke Gachihi is on the front lines of **social justice**, particularly advocating for the rights of those living in

informal settlements. From access to water to the right to housing, Gachihi's work aims to improve the lives of some of Kenya's most marginalized citizens.

Al-Amin Kimathi – Human Rights Advocacy for Terror Suspects

Al-Amin Kimathi has made it his mission to defend the human rights of **terror suspects**—a controversial but vital aspect of justice in a nation grappling with terrorism. Kimathi's advocacy ensures that even those accused of heinous crimes are treated justly under the law.

Lynn Ngugi – Gender Issues, Social Justice Storytelling

With her engaging and emotional storytelling, **Lynn Ngugi** has become a voice for the voiceless, particularly when it comes to **gender issues** and **social justice**. Her online documentaries and interviews bring attention to the struggles of ordinary Kenyans, particularly women, giving them a platform to share their stories.

Ruth Mumbi – Women's Rights, Urban Poor Advocacy

Ruth Mumbi has dedicated her life to advocating for the **rights of women** and the **urban poor**. From fighting for better housing conditions to ensuring women have access to health services, Mumbi's leadership is rooted in her unwavering commitment to justice for marginalized communities.

Jeremiah Matagaro – Youth Advocacy, Environmental Justice

Young, passionate, and dedicated to the cause of **environmental justice, Jeremiah Matagaro** is advocating for sustainable practices while empowering **youth** to take an active role in protecting Kenya's natural resources. His work is helping to shape a future where young Kenyans lead the charge in combating climate change.

Environmental and Sustainable Development

The future of Kenya depends not just on its political leaders but on its environmental defenders. These are the individuals who are working to protect Kenya's natural beauty and promote **sustainability**.

Wangari Maathai – Environmental Conservation, Reforestation

No list of environmental champions would be complete without mentioning **Wangari Maathai**, the woman who literally **planted** the future. Founder of the **Green Belt Movement**, Maathai's work in **reforestation** and **environmental conservation** is legendary. Her efforts to protect forests and empower women through environmental activism earned her the **Nobel Peace Prize**, and her legacy continues to inspire environmental movements across the world.

Phyllis Omido – Environmental Justice, Pollution Control

Known as the **East African Erin Brockovich, Phyllis Omido** is a fierce advocate for **environmental justice**. After discovering that a lead-smelting factory in her community was poisoning residents, she led a successful campaign to have it shut down. Omido's fight against corporate polluters has shown that environmental justice is a critical part of human rights.

Fatuma Abdulkadir Adan – Peace Advocacy Through Sports and Environmental Justice

Fatuma Abdulkadir Adan is using the power of **sports** to promote **peace** and **environmental justice** in Northern Kenya. Her organization, **Horn of Africa Development Initiative (HODI)**, uses football to bring together communities in conflict, while also teaching the importance of conserving natural resources. Adan's unique approach to peacebuilding and environmentalism is a model for how sports can change lives.

Lorna Rutto – Eco-Friendly Products, Plastic Recycling

Tired of seeing Kenya's landscape littered with plastic, **Lorna Rutto** started **EcoPost**, a company that turns plastic waste into eco-friendly fencing posts. Rutto's innovative approach to **plastic recycling** has not only helped reduce pollution but also created jobs, proving that **sustainable development** and economic growth can go hand in hand.

Tony Nyagah – Solar Energy, Sustainable Energy Solutions

Tony Nyagah is helping to solve Kenya's energy crisis through **solar energy solutions**. His company is bringing clean, affordable energy to rural communities that are off the grid, reducing reliance on fossil fuels and promoting sustainable energy practices.

David Kuria – Eco-Friendly Sanitation Solutions

David Kuria is tackling Kenya's sanitation challenges with **eco-friendly toilets**. His company, **Ecotact**, builds sanitation facilities that are environmentally sustainable, while also promoting hygiene in urban and peri-urban areas. Kuria's work is revolutionizing how we think about waste management in densely populated areas.

Evans Wadongo – Solar Energy Products for Rural Areas

At just 19 years old, **Evans Wadongo** invented a solar-powered LED lamp, which has since brought light to thousands of homes in rural Kenya. His work in **solar energy** is giving communities access to clean, affordable lighting, reducing reliance on kerosene lamps, and promoting environmental sustainability.

Matthew Ruto – Waste Management and Recycling

Matthew Ruto is at the forefront of **waste management** and **recycling** in Kenya. His company, **TakaTaka Solutions**, is working to reduce waste by promoting recycling practices in urban areas. Ruto's work is not only cleaning up Nairobi's streets but also creating jobs in the waste management sector.

Trushna Buddhdev-Patel – Handcrafted Footwear Promoting Sustainable Fashion

Trushna Buddhdev-Patel is combining **fashion and sustainability** with her company, **Ikwetta**, which produces handcrafted footwear using eco-friendly materials. By promoting **sustainable fashion**, Buddhdev-Patel is proving that style doesn't have to come at the cost of the environment.

Peter Njonjo – Food Distribution and Sustainable Farming (Twiga Foods)

Through **Twiga Foods**, **Peter Njonjo** is revolutionizing **food distribution** in Kenya by connecting small-scale farmers to markets using a technology-driven supply chain. His work is reducing food waste, improving farmers' incomes, and promoting **sustainable farming** practices across the country.

Catherine Mahugu – Empowering Artisans Through Eco-Friendly Online Marketplace (Soko)

Catherine Mahugu is using technology to empower artisans across Kenya with her online marketplace, **Soko**, which sells eco-friendly, handmade jewelry and crafts. Mahugu's platform is helping artisans reach global markets while promoting **sustainability** in fashion.

Kenyatta Kanyeki – Solar-Powered Solutions for Rural Communities

Kenyatta Kanyeki is focused on bringing **solar power** to rural communities through his company, **Mbegu Solar**. By providing affordable, off-grid energy solutions, Kanyeki is giving communities the tools they need to thrive in a sustainable and environmentally friendly way.

Technology and Innovation

Kenya is often called the **Silicon Savannah** for a reason—its tech innovators are creating groundbreaking solutions that are transforming industries and improving lives. From health tech to fintech, these leaders are driving Kenya's future.

Juliana Rotich – Ushahidi Platform, Tech for Crisis Mapping

Juliana Rotich is a co-founder of **Ushahidi**, the platform that uses crowdsourced data to create crisis maps during natural disasters and political unrest. Her work in **crisis mapping technology** has been used around the world to track and respond to emergencies, making her one of Kenya's most influential tech leaders.

Ken Njoroge – Mobile Banking and Fintech Solutions (Cellulant)

As the co-founder of **Cellulant**, **Ken Njoroge** is a pioneer in **mobile banking** and **fintech** solutions. His company is providing digital payment platforms for businesses and individuals across Africa, revolutionizing how money moves on the continent.

Mark Kaigwa – Digital Marketing and Storytelling (Nendo)

Mark Kaigwa is the founder of **Nendo**, a digital marketing and storytelling firm that helps brands connect with audiences in authentic ways. Kaigwa's work in **digital storytelling** is transforming how businesses engage with consumers, proving that creativity is key to success in the digital age.

Brian Gitta – Non-Invasive Malaria Testing (Matibabu)

Tired of seeing people suffer from **malaria**, **Brian Gitta** invented **Matibabu**, a non-invasive device that tests for malaria without the need for blood samples. Gitta's health tech innovation is improving access to malaria diagnosis and treatment in Kenya and beyond.

Cynthia Wandia – Digital Banking Solutions (Kwara)

Cynthia Wandia is the co-founder of **Kwara**, a digital banking platform designed for credit unions and cooperatives. Her work is making financial services more accessible to low-income individuals, empowering them to save, invest, and grow their wealth.

Eunice Njeri – Ed-Tech Solutions (Zydii)

Eunice Njeri is changing the way Kenyans learn with her **ed-tech platform, Zydii,** which offers affordable online courses on everything from business skills to personal development. Njeri's work is democratizing education and giving Kenyans the tools they need to succeed in a rapidly changing world.

Jihan Abass – Digital-Only Insurance (Griffin Insurance)

Jihan Abass is the founder of **Griffin Insurance**, Kenya's first **digital-only insurance company**. Her innovative approach is making insurance more accessible and affordable, particularly for young people and small businesses.

Valentine Njoroge – Communications Tech (Africa's Talking)

Valentine Njoroge is leading the charge in **communications technology** through **Africa's Talking**, a company that provides digital solutions for developers and businesses across Africa. Njoroge's work is enabling companies to communicate more effectively, driving innovation in the digital economy.

Sam Gichuru – Startup Accelerator (Nailab)
As the founder of **Nailab**, **Sam Gichuru** is helping Kenyan entrepreneurs turn their ideas into successful startups. His **startup accelerator** provides mentorship, funding, and resources to innovators, fostering the next generation of Kenyan tech entrepreneurs.

Ibrahim Gachanja – Ed-Tech and Productivity Platform (AirKlip)

Ibrahim Gachanja is the brains behind **AirKlip**, an ed-tech and productivity platform designed to help students organize their study materials and manage their time more effectively. Gachanja's work is helping students across Kenya achieve academic success through digital tools.

Nekesa Were – Tech Incubation and Innovation Hub (iHub)

As the director of **iHub**, **Nekesa Were** is fostering Kenya's **tech incubation** ecosystem, providing a space for innovators, developers, and entrepreneurs to collaborate and create cutting-edge solutions. iHub has become the heart of Kenya's tech scene, driving innovation in everything from mobile apps to renewable energy.

Anthony Mutua – Renewable Energy Inventions

Anthony Mutua is an innovator in the field of **renewable energy**. His inventions, such as shoes that generate electricity as you walk, are providing creative solutions to Kenya's energy challenges while promoting sustainability.

David Ndung'u – Solar Energy Products (M-Kopa Solar)

As part of the team at **M-Kopa Solar**, **David Ndung'u** is working to bring **solar energy** to rural households in Kenya. By providing affordable solar-powered products, Ndung'u is helping to close the energy gap and promote sustainable development.

Lavender Ochieng – Youth Development and Mentorship (Ongoza)

Through her work with **Ongoza**, **Lavender Ochieng** is mentoring **young entrepreneurs** and helping them develop the skills they need to build successful businesses. Ochieng's leadership is empowering Kenya's youth to take

charge of their futures and create opportunities for
themselves.

Leshan Juma – Solar-Powered Off-Grid Energy Solutions (Mbegu Solar)

Leshan Juma is bringing clean energy to off-grid
communities through his company, **Mbegu Solar**. By
providing affordable, **solar-powered energy solutions**,
Juma is helping to improve the quality of life for rural
Kenyans while promoting environmental sustainability.

Healthcare

Kenya's healthcare system is in need of innovative
solutions, and these leaders are stepping up to the
challenge. From affordable healthcare to nutrition and
health tech, they're improving lives and transforming the
healthcare landscape.

Dr. Maxwell Okoth – Affordable Healthcare (Ruai Family Hospital)

Dr. Maxwell Okoth is on a mission to make **affordable
healthcare** accessible to all Kenyans. Through his chain of
Ruai Family Hospitals, Okoth is bringing quality
healthcare to underserved communities, ensuring that no
one is left behind when it comes to medical care.

Wawira Njiru – Nutrition and Health for School Children (Food for Education)

Wawira Njiru is tackling **child malnutrition** through her
organization, **Food for Education**, which provides
nutritious meals to schoolchildren in underserved areas.

Njiru's work is improving academic performance and health outcomes for thousands of children, proving that good nutrition is the foundation of a brighter future.

Brian Gitta – Health Tech for Malaria Testing (Matibabu)

We've already mentioned **Brian Gitta** and his non-invasive malaria testing device, **Matibabu**, but it bears repeating: Gitta's health tech innovation is revolutionizing the way malaria is diagnosed, making it easier, faster, and more affordable for people in malaria-prone areas to get tested and treated.

Nelly Tuikong – Locally Made Beauty Products for African Skin (Pauline Cosmetics)

Nelly Tuikong is the founder of **Pauline Cosmetics**, a beauty brand that creates products specifically for **African skin**. By focusing on the unique needs of African women, Tuikong is promoting confidence, self-care, and beauty standards that reflect the diversity of the continent.

Sheila Waruguru – Empowering Women in Healthcare (Nailab Garments)

Through her work at **Nailab Garments**, **Sheila Waruguru** is empowering women in the healthcare industry by providing affordable, high-quality **medical garments**. Waruguru's work is creating jobs and improving healthcare standards in Kenya.

Peter Njonjo – Food Security and Distribution (Twiga Foods)

We've already covered **Peter Njonjo** in the environmental section, but his work in **food security** and distribution through **Twiga Foods** is also contributing to the healthcare sector by ensuring that Kenyans have access to fresh, nutritious food. Njonjo's company is bridging the gap between small-scale farmers and consumers, reducing food waste and improving food security in Kenya.

Ken Njoroge – Financial Solutions for Health and Banking (Cellulant)

While we've discussed **Ken Njoroge** in the fintech section, his work also extends to **healthcare financing**. Through **Cellulant**, Njoroge is helping to provide financial solutions that make healthcare more affordable and accessible, especially for those in underserved areas.

Youth Empowerment and Education

Kenya's youth are the future, and these leaders are ensuring that they have the tools, resources, and mentorship they need to succeed.

Amos Mwago – Youth Advocacy, Education, and Entrepreneurship

Amos Mwago is a passionate advocate for **youth empowerment**, focusing on education and entrepreneurship as key drivers of change. His work ensures that young people have the skills and opportunities they need to build successful futures.

Eunice Njeri – Skills Development Through Online Learning Platforms (Zydii)

Eunice Njeri is once again leading the charge in **online education** with her platform, **Zydii**, which offers courses in everything from business skills to personal development. Njeri's work is making education more accessible and empowering young Kenyans to take control of their learning.

Elizabeth Gikebe – Agricultural Entrepreneurship and Food Security (Mhogo Foods)

Elizabeth Gikebe is tackling **food security** through her company, **Mhogo Foods**, which focuses on producing affordable, nutritious cassava products. Gikebe's work is empowering smallholder farmers and ensuring that Kenyans have access to sustainable food sources.

Sheilah Birgen – Innovators Mentorship (The Innovators Society)

Through **The Innovators Society**, **Sheilah Birgen** is mentoring **young innovators**, helping them develop their ideas into successful businesses. Birgen's work is fostering a culture of creativity and entrepreneurship among Kenya's youth.

Joel Macharia – Financial Education Platform (Abacus)

Joel Macharia is the founder of **Abacus**, a financial education platform that helps young people learn about saving, investing, and managing their money. Macharia's work is empowering a new generation of financially literate Kenyans.

Lynn Ngugi – Social Justice Storytelling and Youth Empowerment

Lynn Ngugi is once again leading the charge in **social justice storytelling**, using her platform to give young people a voice and empower them to become advocates for change. Ngugi's work is inspiring youth to get involved in social justice issues and take a stand for what they believe in.

Nekesa Were – Incubation for Young Tech Innovators (iHub)

As we've already mentioned, **Nekesa Were** is at the helm of **iHub**, providing a space for **young tech innovators** to collaborate, develop their ideas, and create solutions that will shape the future of Kenya's tech industry.

Eunice Njeri – Online Education Platform (Zydii)

Once again, **Eunice Njeri** is making waves in **online education** with her platform, **Zydii**, which is providing young Kenyans with the tools they need to succeed in a rapidly changing world.

Sophie Gichugu – Education Innovation and Technology Integration (Mount Kenya Academy)

Sophie Gichugu is leading the charge in **education innovation**, using technology to improve learning outcomes at **Mount Kenya Academy**. Gichugu's work is ensuring that Kenyan students have access to the best educational tools and resources available.

Faith Rono – Agricultural Innovations to Empower Smallholder Farmers (AfriGreen Ventures)

Faith Rono is using **agricultural innovations** to empower **smallholder farmers** through her company, **AfriGreen Ventures**. Rono's work is improving agricultural productivity and food security, while also providing farmers with the tools they need to succeed.

Entrepreneurship and Business Development

Kenya's entrepreneurial spirit is alive and well, thanks to these leaders who are building businesses, creating jobs, and driving economic growth.

Eric Kinoti – Manufacturing (Shade Systems EA)

Eric Kinoti is a self-made entrepreneur who founded **Shade Systems EA**, a company that manufactures tents and shades for events and businesses. Kinoti's entrepreneurial journey is a testament to the power of hard work, resilience, and innovation in business.

Tabitha Karanja – Beverage Industry (Keroche Breweries)

As the founder of **Keroche Breweries**, **Tabitha Karanja** is one of Kenya's most successful female entrepreneurs.

Her company is a trailblazer in the **beverage industry**, and Karanja's leadership has challenged the dominance of international players in the market.

Njeri Rionge – Affordable Internet Services (Wananchi Online)

Njeri Rionge is a pioneer in **affordable internet services** in Kenya. As the co-founder of **Wananchi Online**, she has played a key role in expanding internet access across East Africa, making it possible for more people to connect and grow in the digital age.

Joel Macharia – Investment Solutions (Abacus)

Once again, **Joel Macharia** is leading the way in **investment solutions** with **Abacus**, which provides young Kenyans with the knowledge and tools they need to build wealth through investing.

Eric Kinoti – Manufacturing Tents and Related Products (Shade Systems EA)

We've already mentioned **Eric Kinoti**, but it bears repeating: his company, **Shade Systems EA**, is revolutionizing the **manufacturing industry** in Kenya, providing high-quality products that meet the needs of businesses and consumers alike.

Eugene Mbugua – Media and Entertainment (Young Rich Television Ltd)

Eugene Mbugua is shaking up the **media and entertainment industry** with his company, **Young Rich Television Ltd**, which produces popular reality TV shows that highlight Kenya's growing middle class. Mbugua's work is changing the narrative around wealth, success, and entrepreneurship in Kenya.

Bryan Kariuki – Practical Business Education (Hustla MBA)

Through his platform, **Hustla MBA**, **Bryan Kariuki** is providing **practical business education** to young entrepreneurs, helping them develop the skills they need to succeed in Kenya's competitive business environment.

Nelly Tuikong – Cosmetics for African Women (Pauline Cosmetics)

Once again, **Nelly Tuikong** is making waves in the **cosmetics industry** with her brand, **Pauline Cosmetics**, which is creating products specifically for **African women**. Tuikong's business is empowering women to feel confident in their own skin, while also providing jobs and economic opportunities.

Brenda Wairimu – Fashion Business (Taji Clothing)

Brenda Wairimu is using her platform as a fashion designer and entrepreneur to promote **local production** and **sustainable fashion** through her brand, **Taji Clothing**. Wairimu's work is creating jobs and promoting Kenya's fashion industry on the global stage.

Susan Wanjiru – Garment Manufacturing (Nailab Garments)

As the founder of **Nailab Garments**, **Susan Wanjiru** is leading the way in **garment manufacturing** in Kenya. Her company is creating jobs, promoting local production, and improving access to high-quality, affordable clothing.

Jihan Abass – Digital Insurance Solutions (Griffin Insurance)

Once again, **Jihan Abass** is changing the game with **Griffin Insurance**, Kenya's first **digital-only insurance company**. Abass's work is making insurance more accessible and affordable for young people and small businesses, driving innovation in the insurance industry.

Fashion, Media, and Creative Arts

Kenya's **fashion and creative arts** scene is thriving, thanks to leaders who are using their talents to make a difference in the world.

Caroline Mutoko – Gender Advocacy and Media Influence

As a prominent media personality, **Caroline Mutoko** has used her platform to advocate for **gender equality** and **women's empowerment**. Mutoko's influence in the media industry is shaping public perceptions of women's roles in society and promoting gender equity in the workplace.

Ndungi Githuku – Filmmaking and Cultural Storytelling

Ndungi Githuku is a filmmaker and cultural storyteller who is using his art to showcase Kenya's rich history and traditions. Githuku's work in **filmmaking** is promoting **cultural preservation** and encouraging younger generations to take pride in their heritage.

Juliana Rotich – Tech and Digital Storytelling

As we've mentioned, **Juliana Rotich** is a leader in **tech innovation**, but her work in **digital storytelling** is also transforming how we tell stories in the digital age. Through her platform, **Ushahidi**, Rotich is helping people share their experiences and track events in real-time, changing the way we document history.

Tatiana Karanja – Sustainable Baby Products (Mama Olive)

Tatiana Karanja is the founder of **Mama Olive**, a company that produces **sustainable baby products** made from eco-friendly materials. Karanja's work is promoting sustainability in parenting, while also creating jobs and reducing waste.

Brenda Wairimu – Fashion Design and Local Production (Taji Clothing)

Once again, **Brenda Wairimu** is using her platform in the **fashion industry** to promote local production and sustainable practices. Wairimu's work is empowering young fashion designers and creating economic opportunities in Kenya's growing fashion scene.

Megan Mukuria – Empowering Young Girls Through Sanitary Products (ZanaAfrica)

Megan Mukuria is the founder of **ZanaAfrica**, a company that produces **affordable sanitary products** for young girls. Mukuria's work is empowering girls to stay in school and achieve their full potential, while also promoting menstrual health and hygiene.

Dr. Njoki Ngumi – Creative Arts and Media (The Nest Collective)

Dr. Njoki Ngumi is a key member of **The Nest Collective**, a group of artists and filmmakers who are using their platform to challenge social norms and push for change. Ngumi's work in **creative arts and media** is inspiring a new generation of artists to use their talents for social justice.

Sheila Waruguru – Fashion for Job Creation (Black & White Denim)

As the founder of **Black & White Denim, Sheila Waruguru** is using fashion to create jobs and promote sustainable practices in the garment industry. Waruguru's work is empowering women to take control of their economic futures, while also promoting environmentally friendly production methods.

Trushna Buddhdev-Patel – Fashion and Craftsmanship (Ikwetta)

Once again, **Trushna Buddhdev-Patel** is promoting **fashion and craftsmanship** through her company, **Ikwetta**, which produces handcrafted footwear using eco-friendly materials. Buddhdev-Patel's work is creating jobs, promoting sustainability, and showcasing Kenya's rich tradition of craftsmanship to the world.

Strengthening the Justice System – Upholding the Rule of Law for All

Kenya's justice system is a bit like a well-meaning uncle at a family reunion: sometimes late, often confused, but occasionally capable of greatness when the stars align. For years, the Kenyan public has had a complicated relationship with the judiciary—one part respect, one part frustration, and maybe even a dash of disbelief when rulings don't seem to make sense. But here's the thing: despite all the courtroom drama, long delays, and notorious bribery jokes that plague our justice system, one truth stands tall—without a strong, efficient, and fair judiciary, there can be no real justice, no peace, and certainly no national integrity.

Strengthening Kenya's justice system is a task of epic proportions, akin to trying to solve Nairobi's traffic problem or convincing a boda boda rider to follow traffic rules. It's about more than just fancy courtrooms and robed judges. It's about ensuring that every Kenyan, whether they live in a mansion in Runda or a mud hut in Turkana, can access justice when they need it. It's about eliminating impunity, holding the powerful accountable, and ensuring that the law applies equally to all, whether you're a politician, a matatu driver, or an ordinary citizen caught up in a land dispute.

In this chapter, we'll dive deep into the world of Kenya's justice system—its quirks, its shortcomings, its occasional flashes of brilliance, and why strengthening it is absolutely crucial for Kenya's future. And because this is Kenya, expect a lot of laughter along the way, because let's face it: some of the things that happen in court could easily be mistaken for plotlines from a comedy show.

The Courtroom Chronicles: Where Drama Meets Delays

Picture this: you're in a courtroom in Nairobi, and the atmosphere is as tense as a World Cup final. The case being heard is a high-profile corruption scandal involving billions of shillings. The lawyers are decked out in crisp suits, the judge is trying to maintain order, and the public gallery is packed with curious onlookers, journalists, and the defendant's relatives who insist on bringing the largest thermos of tea known to mankind.

And then, just when the proceedings are getting interesting, the lawyer for the defense stands up and announces that he needs more time to "prepare." The judge sighs, the public groans, and the case is adjourned—again. It's not unusual for cases in Kenya to drag on for years, sometimes decades, as lawyers pull every trick in the book to delay proceedings. Need a medical note excusing your absence? No problem. Want to argue about a minor technicality for hours? Go ahead. The system, as it currently stands, seems to favor those with the most time, money, and connections.

This, my friends, is the state of many Kenyan courtrooms: a delightful mix of drama, delay, and legal gymnastics that could leave even the most patient soul questioning the very fabric of reality. But behind the absurdity is a very real problem—the slow pace of justice in Kenya is eroding public confidence in the judiciary. When cases involving ordinary Kenyans are delayed for years, when murder trials are postponed so often that people forget the names of the victims, when land disputes outlast the people fighting over the land, it's clear that something is broken.

Speeding up Kenya's justice system is not just about efficiency—it's about restoring faith in the rule of law. It's about making sure that justice delayed is not justice denied. And to achieve that, we need more judges, better case management systems, and, perhaps, a nationwide campaign to encourage lawyers to stop using "I was sick" as their go-to excuse for every adjournment request.

The Bizarre Bribery Circus: How Much for Your Freedom?

Ah, bribery—the not-so-secret ingredient in the Kenyan justice system. If you've ever spent time in a Kenyan court, you've probably heard the jokes: *"Justice is blind, but with the right bribe, it gets 20/20 vision."* It's not just a joke, though—it's a reality that many Kenyans face when navigating the justice system, and it's one of the biggest barriers to true justice.

From the traffic cop who subtly asks for "kitu kidogo" to let you off the hook for a minor offense, to the court clerk who mysteriously loses your file unless you "appreciate" their efforts, bribery in the justice system is as common as Nairobi traffic jams. And while it's easy to laugh about it (because let's be honest, the bribery stories are often ridiculous), it's no laughing matter. Bribery erodes trust in the judiciary, making it impossible for ordinary Kenyans to believe that they can get a fair hearing without paying someone off.

But what happens when even judges and lawyers are caught in bribery scandals? Well, then you get the infamous case of the "chicken-gate" scandal, where bribes were reportedly referred to as "chicken" in coded conversations. It's like something out of a spy movie, except it's real life, and it's happening in the very institutions that are supposed to uphold justice.

To tackle this, Kenya's judiciary needs a complete culture shift. Anti-corruption efforts have to go beyond the occasional high-profile arrests and reach into the everyday functioning of courts, police stations, and legal offices. Judges and judicial officers must be held to the highest standards of integrity, and Kenyans need to feel confident that when they walk into a courtroom, they won't need to slip someone an envelope just to have their case heard. The Judiciary's **Judicial Service Commission (JSC)** has made strides in this regard, with efforts to expose and root out corrupt judges, but there's still a long way to go before the rot is fully cleared.

The Power Imbalance: Justice for the Rich, Injustice for the Poor

Let's be honest: if you're wealthy or well-connected in Kenya, you're likely to have a smoother experience with the justice system than if you're poor and unknown. It's the unspoken truth that everyone knows but no one wants to talk about. The gap between the haves and the have-nots is nowhere more evident than in the courtroom, where those who can afford the best lawyers, pull the right strings, and pay off the right people often come out on top.

Meanwhile, for the average Kenyan, accessing justice can feel like climbing Mount Kenya in flip-flops. Legal fees are exorbitant, cases take forever, and public defenders (if you're lucky enough to get one) are often overworked and under-resourced. The power imbalance is stark, and it creates a system where the rich can delay or avoid justice entirely, while the poor are left languishing in remand for months, sometimes years, awaiting trial.

Take the example of the countless Kenyans who are arrested for minor offenses—hawkers selling vegetables without a permit, boda boda riders who park in the wrong spot—and end up stuck in remand because they can't afford bail. In contrast, wealthy individuals facing charges of fraud, corruption, or worse are often granted bail in amounts that would make most Kenyans' jaws drop. It's not that the law is different for the rich and poor, but it's applied differently based on how deep your pockets are.

Eliminating this power imbalance is key to strengthening Kenya's justice system. It starts with making legal aid more accessible to those who need it most. The government's **National Legal Aid Service (NLAS)** is a step in the right direction, but the program needs more funding and better outreach, especially in rural areas where many Kenyans don't even know they have the right to a lawyer. It's also about simplifying the legal process so that ordinary Kenyans can understand and navigate the system without needing a law degree.

Judiciary Reforms: A Few Steps Forward, and a Few Back

Kenya's judiciary has undergone several reforms in recent years, with some success. The **2010 Constitution** brought about significant changes aimed at enhancing the independence of the judiciary and promoting accountability. The introduction of the **Judiciary Transformation Framework (JTF)** under former Chief Justice **Willy Mutunga** was a major step forward, emphasizing transparency, efficiency, and access to justice for all Kenyans. The reforms were met with widespread optimism, and for a while, it seemed like the judiciary was finally on track to becoming a pillar of justice.

But like any good Kenyan story, the road to success has not been smooth. Despite the reforms, the judiciary still faces numerous challenges, including a massive backlog of cases, underfunding, and accusations of corruption. The 2017 presidential election dispute, which saw the Supreme Court annul the election results, showed that the judiciary could be bold and independent. However, the aftermath also revealed how deeply political pressure can impact the judiciary's ability to function without interference.

The ongoing struggle to maintain the judiciary's independence is critical to upholding the rule of law. Judges must be able to make decisions based on the law, not on political pressure or personal gain. Strengthening the judiciary means continuing the work of reforming court systems, improving the working conditions of judges and magistrates, and ensuring that the courts are accessible to all Kenyans, regardless of their social or economic status.

The Role of Technology: From File-Fishing to Digital Justice

Now, let's take a moment to talk about one of the most frustrating aspects of Kenya's justice system—lost files. There's a joke in Kenya that if you want your court case to disappear, all you have to do is "lose" the file. In reality, the issue of missing court documents is a serious one, and it has led to countless delays in the administration of justice. In some cases, files have been "lost" so many times that the parties involved simply give up, tired of showing up to court only to hear, "We're still looking for your file."

Enter technology. Kenya's judiciary has started to embrace digital solutions in an effort to streamline the court process and eliminate the inefficiencies that come with mountains of paperwork. The introduction of the **e-filing system** is a game-changer, allowing lawyers to file cases online and reducing the need for endless trips to court registries.

Similarly, the **Kenya Law Reports website** has made it easier for lawyers, judges, and the public to access legal information and case law without needing to dig through dusty shelves of law books.

But while these technological advancements are a step in the right direction, there's still a long way to go. Internet access remains limited in many parts of the country, and the e-filing system, while promising, has faced its fair share of teething problems. However, the potential for technology to transform Kenya's justice system is enormous. Imagine a future where you can attend court hearings via Zoom from your shamba, or where AI-powered tools help judges make faster, fairer decisions. It sounds far-fetched now, but so did mobile banking once upon a time.

Conclusion: Justice for All—A Work in Progress

Strengthening Kenya's justice system is not a luxury—it's a necessity. Without an efficient and fair judiciary, Kenya cannot uphold the rule of law, eliminate impunity, or support national integrity and peace. The road ahead is long, and there will undoubtedly be bumps, detours, and the occasional lost file. But if we can reform the courts, eliminate corruption, speed up the judicial process, and make justice accessible to all Kenyans, then we will have built a foundation upon which the country can truly thrive.

So, here's to a future where justice is no longer a distant dream but a reality for every Kenyan. A future where court cases don't drag on for decades, where bribery is a thing of the past, and where the rule of law is upheld for all, regardless of wealth, status, or connections. It may sound like a tall order, but in the words of a famous Kenyan proverb, *"Haba na haba hujaza kibaba"*—little by little, we will fill the pot. And that pot? It's filled with justice, fairness, and maybe even a few good jokes along the way.

KEYPOINTS AND SUMMARY

Kenya's Potential and Challenges: Beautiful landscapes and potential hindered by corruption, inefficiency, and chaotic traffic.

Corruption's Impact: Pervasive corruption affects everyday life and public services, but can be eliminated.

Vision for Change: A Kenya where bribes are outdated, public services are efficient, and governance is transparent.

Accountability: Change starts with personal responsibility—rejecting corruption and demanding better leadership.

Future Vision: Functional transport, merit-based politics, and public services without bribery.

Cultural Transformation: A shift toward integrity, innovation, and collective responsibility can unlock Kenya's full potential.

Corruption's Ubiquity: Corruption pervades all levels of society, nurtured by cultural norms and systemic flaws.

Roots of Corruption: Begins with small bribes and grows into a culture of shortcuts and greed.

Promoting Accountability: Change starts with individuals rejecting corruption and promoting accountability in everyday actions.

Citizens' Power: Citizens must demand transparency, vote wisely, and hold leaders accountable.

Successful Examples: Countries like Singapore, Rwanda, and Georgia have successfully reduced corruption through strict laws and cultural change.

Integrity Begins with Us: Combating corruption requires collective action, starting with everyday integrity.

Public Service Issues: Public service has become self-serving, with inefficiency and bribery common.

True Meaning of Public Service: It should focus on serving the public with integrity and dedication.
Celebrating Ethical Leaders: Selfless leaders like Wangari Maathai and John Githongo exemplify ethical governance.
Youth Leadership: Encouraging youth to view leadership as a path to national transformation.
Merit-Based System: Calls for a system that rewards merit, not connections, to improve governance.
Call to Action: Reclaim public service by demanding transparency, integrity, and accountability.

Leadership for the Future – Nurturing the Next Generation of Kenyan Leaders
Servant Leadership: Kenyan leadership should shift from self-serving elites to servant leadership focused on uplifting society and solving problems.
Youth and New Leaders: Emerging leaders are advocating for justice, environmental conservation, technology, healthcare, and more.

Social Justice, Human Rights, and Governance
1. **Key Figures**:
    Boniface Mwangi: A vocal activist against corruption and human rights abuses.
    Okiya Omtatah: Legal crusader against corruption.
    John Githongo: Advocate for transparency in governance.

Environmental and Sustainable Development
Wangari Maathai: Environmental conservation pioneer.
Lorna Rutto: Innovator in plastic recycling, promoting eco-friendly practices.
Tony Nyagah: Solar energy advocate for rural Kenya.

Technology and Innovation

Juliana Rotich: Co-founder of Ushahidi, utilizing tech for crisis mapping.
Ken Njoroge: Pioneer in mobile banking (Cellulant).
Brian Gitta: Innovator in non-invasive malaria testing (Matibabu).

Healthcare Innovation
Dr. Maxwell Okoth: Founder of Ruai Family Hospitals, promoting affordable healthcare.
Wawira Njiru: Tackling child malnutrition through Food for Education.
Nelly Tuikong: Promotes African beauty products through Pauline Cosmetics.

Youth Empowerment and Education
Amos Mwago: Advocate for youth education and entrepreneurship.
Eunice Njeri: Providing affordable online education through Zydii.

Entrepreneurship and Business Development
Tabitha Karanja: Founder of Keroche Breweries, breaking barriers in the beverage industry.
Eric Kinoti: Entrepreneur leading in manufacturing (Shade Systems EA).

Fashion, Media, and Creative Arts
Caroline Mutoko: Media influence and gender advocacy.
Ndungi Githuku: Cultural storytelling through filmmaking.
Trushna Buddhdev-Patel: Sustainable fashion and craftsmanship.
These leaders represent a shift towards transparency, innovation, and sustainable development in Kenya, fostering a brighter future across multiple sectors.

Justice System Challenges: Kenya's judiciary is plagued by delays, bribery, and inefficiencies, eroding public trust.
Delays in Courts: High-profile cases often drag on for years, favoring those with resources, while ordinary Kenyans face long waits for justice.
Widespread Bribery: Corruption within the justice system, from police to judges, undermines fairness, making bribery a common barrier to justice.
Power Imbalance: Wealthy individuals often receive preferential treatment, while the poor struggle to access legal aid or fair hearings.
Judiciary Reforms: Efforts like the 2010 Constitution and Judiciary Transformation Framework have made progress but face political pressure and resource challenges.

Role of Technology: Digital solutions like e-filing can reduce inefficiencies but need broader implementation.
Path Forward: Strengthening the judiciary is crucial for upholding the rule of law, eliminating corruption, and ensuring justice for all Kenyans.

Empowering Citizens: Education, Health, and Social Progress

Learning for Life – The Role of Education in Transforming Kenya

Ladies and gentlemen, boys and girls, and esteemed readers who probably clicked on this chapter by mistake because they thought it was about a Netflix series—welcome! Today, we're diving deep into a topic that's as essential as your daily cup of chai (or coffee, if you're one of those fancy types): **education.**

Yes, education—the thing we all took for granted when we were kids, mostly because it meant waking up early, memorizing things like algebra, and staring blankly at teachers who seemed to think we all had the intellectual capacities of Einstein. But, as we grew older and perhaps realized that being a famous rapper or footballer wasn't in the cards, we began to see that education, while not as glamorous as celebrity life, is indeed the real deal when it comes to transforming lives.

So, grab your metaphorical schoolbags and let's get started on a journey that shows why education isn't just important; it's downright essential for Kenya's future.

Education as a Tool for Social Mobility and National Progress

Let's start with a fun fact. Did you know that education is like the original elevator? Not the kind with buttons and soothing elevator music (although we could use some of that), but the kind that lifts people from the ground floor of poverty and takes them all the way up to the penthouse suite of opportunity. For real, education is the one tool that has the power to move someone from "kufunga mitumba" on the street to giving TED Talks on global stages.

Consider this: You're a young boy or girl in a rural village, where the only thing in abundance is dust. But then, thanks to a local school with dedicated teachers (shoutout to the teachers who work magic despite sometimes earning less than the local boda boda riders), you get an education. Next thing you know, you're off to university, studying engineering, medicine, or computer science. A few years later, you've invented the next mobile app or are treating patients in a state-of-the-art hospital. And just like that, you've not only transformed your life, but you've also become a contributing member of Kenya's growth story. Pretty wild, huh?

That's what education does: it turns ordinary people into extraordinary contributors to national progress. It doesn't matter where you start—whether you were born in the glitzy streets of Nairobi or in a village where goats outnumber people—education can be the key that unlocks your future.

Promoting Lifelong Learning and Vocational Skills

Now, let's get something straight: Education isn't just about sitting in a classroom, staring at blackboards (or whiteboards, if your school's fancy like that). It's not about passing exams just to forget everything two weeks later (although we've all been there). Education is **lifelong**. Yes, lifelong—as in, it never stops. I know, I know—you probably just got flashbacks of your school principal saying, "Learning is a lifelong process," and you rolled your eyes. But hear me out.

Lifelong learning is the new black, the hottest trend that never goes out of style. It's the secret sauce behind staying relevant in a world where technology changes faster than a politician's promises during campaign season. Whether you're 18 or 80, the key to surviving and thriving is constantly learning something new—whether it's a language, a new skill, or how to use TikTok without looking like an awkward uncle at a wedding.

But here's the kicker: Kenya needs to promote **vocational skills** just as much as formal education. Not everyone is going to be a doctor, lawyer, or accountant (although, if that's your thing, more power to you). We also need plumbers, electricians, carpenters, chefs, welders, and, for heaven's sake, competent boda boda mechanics. Have you ever had a boda boda break down in the middle of nowhere and the nearest mechanic tells you, "Ah, I can fix this in 10 minutes," only for him to disappear for two hours? It's a crisis, people.

Vocational skills are the backbone of any thriving economy. In Germany, vocational education is so serious that apprenticeships are more sought after than some university degrees. Why? Because practical skills don't just help individuals earn a living; they drive innovation and development. Kenya could take a page from this book. Imagine a world where a young man or woman who couldn't afford university starts a successful plumbing business and becomes a millionaire. It's possible, but only if we stop looking down on vocational training and start treating it like the gold mine it truly is.

How to Bridge the Gap Between Urban and Rural Education

Ah, the great divide—urban vs. rural education. It's like Nairobi and upcountry are living on two different planets. In one universe, you've got city schools with computer labs, libraries, extracurricular programs, and students who know what Wi-Fi is by the time they're in kindergarten. In the other universe, you've got rural schools where students are sharing one textbook among five people, classrooms double as chicken coops on weekends, and the only form of "technology" is a chalkboard that's been around since the 1980s.

How do we bridge this gap? Glad you asked.
First, **infrastructure, infrastructure, infrastructure!** You know how they say location is everything in real estate? Well, infrastructure is everything in education. The first step is ensuring that rural schools have the basics— functional classrooms, desks, textbooks, and yes, even that luxury we call electricity. Because let's be honest: it's hard to focus on math problems when you're sitting on the floor, swatting flies, and trying to squint at a blackboard in the dim light of a dusty classroom.

But it's not just about buildings and textbooks. **Teacher training and support** is crucial. There are thousands of rural schools where teachers are doing incredible work under impossible conditions, but they need better training and resources. Let's equip teachers with the tools they need to not only teach but inspire. After all, education isn't just about facts and figures—it's about shaping minds and encouraging dreams.

And then there's the great equalizer—**technology**. Now, before you roll your eyes and say, "We can't even get clean water to some of these schools, and now you want to talk about laptops," hear me out. There are low-cost solutions out there—solar-powered digital devices, e-learning platforms that don't need Wi-Fi, mobile libraries, and radio lessons that have worked in other countries facing similar challenges. If a kid in a village can access the same learning resources as a kid in the city, we're halfway to closing the gap. Education is the great equalizer, but we need to make it accessible to everyone, no matter where they live.

Innovative Educational Initiatives to Inspire

Now that we've painted a picture of what needs to be done, let's look at some **real-life initiatives** that are already making waves in Kenya and beyond. Because yes, despite all the challenges, there are some bright sparks out there that should inspire us all.

1. The M-Pesa Foundation Academy

First up, let's talk about the **M-Pesa Foundation Academy**, a game-changer in the world of secondary education. This isn't your average high school—it's a state-of-the-art institution that offers a world-class education to gifted but financially disadvantaged students from across Kenya. The academy blends academics, leadership training, and entrepreneurship, preparing its students to be future leaders and innovators. With facilities that rival some universities, these students have access to resources most could only dream of.

But here's what's cool—this isn't just about academic excellence. It's about giving students the tools to transform their communities once they graduate. The academy emphasizes social entrepreneurship, meaning students aren't just learning for their own benefit—they're being equipped to lift others up as well. It's like killing two birds with one stone, except these birds are education and community development, and no actual birds are harmed. Win-win.

2. Bridge International Academies

Next on the list is **Bridge International Academies**, a
network of low-cost private schools that's taking education
to the people—literally. With a mission to provide quality
education at an affordable price, Bridge Academies use
technology to deliver lessons, monitor student progress,
and ensure accountability. Teachers are equipped with
tablets that guide them through each lesson, ensuring that
quality remains consistent across all schools. The result? A
model that delivers affordable, high-quality education to
students in underserved areas.

Bridge International Academies are particularly impressive
because they've cracked the code of providing good
education on a budget. It's like getting a 5-star meal at a
chapati stand price. Who wouldn't want that?

3. AkiraChix

Now, let's talk about an initiative that's empowering the
next generation of women tech leaders in Kenya—
AkiraChix. AkiraChix is all about training young women
in coding, software development, and entrepreneurship.
This non-profit organization was started to address the
gender gap in the tech industry, and boy, are they doing a
fantastic job.

AkiraChix doesn't just teach girls to code—they mentor
them, provide job placements, and create a supportive
community of women who are changing the face of tech in
Africa. These women aren't just learning tech skills—
they're getting the tools to build a future where they don't
just participate in the economy—they shape it. And with

women like that in charge, I'd say Kenya's future is looking pretty bright.

Conclusion: The Future of Education in Kenya

So, what's the takeaway here, dear reader? Education is the most powerful tool we have to transform Kenya. It's the elevator that can take people from poverty to prosperity, the glue that can bridge the gap between urban and rural areas, and the fuel that powers national progress.

But education doesn't stop after you've finished school—it's a lifelong process. Whether it's vocational skills, tech training, or simply the desire to keep learning something new every day, education is the gift that keeps on giving.

Let's make sure every child, whether they're in Nairobi or the most remote corner of Kenya, has access to the tools and resources they need to succeed. Let's invest in our teachers, our schools, and our communities. Because when we do, we're not just building a better future for our children—we're building a better future for our country.

And who knows? Maybe one day, the kids learning under trees today will be the ones leading us into a future we can all be proud of. Now, wouldn't that be something to celebrate?

Health Is Wealth – Building a Culture of Health and Wellness

Ladies, gentlemen, and all health-conscious (and not-so-health-conscious) Kenyans, gather 'round! It's time we have **the talk**. No, not that talk—we're diving into something far more important than awkward birds-and-bees discussions. We're talking about **health**, the one thing everyone wants but few people truly take care of until it's too late. You see, if there's one thing we've all heard at some point in our lives, it's that **health is wealth**, but for some reason, we still treat our bodies like they're indestructible tuk-tuks that can keep running no matter how much junk we throw at them.

Well, buckle up, because we're about to take a ride through the world of **health and wellness**—and trust me, we're going to do it with plenty of laughs, because if we can't laugh at our bad health habits, how else are we supposed to deal with them? In this chapter, we'll explore how we can shift from reactive to preventive healthcare (yes, that means fewer panic trips to the ER), how promoting mental health awareness can change lives, why a clean environment is like a miracle drug, and how we can build local health systems that actually work. So grab your fruit smoothie (or at least pretend you're drinking one), and let's get started.

Shifting from Reactive to Preventive Healthcare

Let's start with the basics: **Why is it that we only care about our health when it's in crisis mode?** It's like we treat our bodies the same way we treat our cars. We ignore that strange noise coming from the engine for months until one day, smoke starts billowing out of the hood, and suddenly we're running to the mechanic like, "Please fix this, I swear I'll never skip an oil change again!"

In Kenya, we've perfected the art of **reactive healthcare**. We wait until something is very, very wrong before we go to the doctor. Chest pains? "Ah, it's probably just indigestion." Fever? "I'll sleep it off." Persistent headaches? "Must be stress." And don't even get me started on the old "Google diagnosis" routine. One quick search for a sore throat and suddenly you're convinced you have a rare tropical disease last seen in the Amazon rainforest.

But here's the deal: **reactive healthcare is like trying to build a house after the roof has already collapsed**. We need to shift to **preventive healthcare**, which is basically the healthcare equivalent of "an apple a day keeps the doctor away"—except it's more like, "Regular check-ups, a balanced diet, and exercise keep the hospital bills away."

Preventive healthcare is about being proactive. It's about **getting ahead of the problem** instead of waiting for it to explode in your face. Think of it like this: instead of waiting for your car's engine to die, why not just take it in for regular maintenance? The same goes for your body— regular check-ups, vaccinations, screenings, and a commitment to living a healthy lifestyle can help you avoid major health crises down the road.

And guess what? **Preventive healthcare is cheaper**. That's right—taking care of yourself now means fewer medical bills later. And who doesn't love saving money? It's the closest thing to winning the lottery, except you're winning by not having to spend half your salary on medications with names you can't pronounce.

Promoting Mental Health Awareness in Communities

Now, let's talk about something that makes people uncomfortable—**mental health**. I know, I know, it's not exactly the kind of conversation you'd bring up at the dinner table with your grandparents, but hear me out: **mental health is just as important as physical health**, and if we don't start taking it seriously, we're all going to be in trouble.

In Kenya, mental health is still shrouded in stigma. Too often, when someone is struggling with depression, anxiety, or any other mental health issue, they're told to "pray about it" or "toughen up." Let me be clear: while prayer and strength are important, **they're not a substitute for proper mental healthcare**. You wouldn't tell someone with a broken leg to just "walk it off," would you? So why do we do this with mental health?

It's time to change the narrative. **Mental health is health**, and we need to start treating it that way. This means **raising awareness in our communities**, breaking the stigma, and creating spaces where people feel comfortable talking about their mental health struggles without being judged.

Imagine a world where you could tell someone you're feeling overwhelmed or anxious, and instead of hearing, "It's all in your head," they say, "I understand, let's talk about it." Imagine a Kenya where we have **community mental health centers** that offer affordable therapy, support groups, and mental health education programs. Imagine a society where people are encouraged to prioritize their mental well-being, just like they would with their physical health.

Sound impossible? It's not. It starts with us. We need to start **having these conversations**, supporting those who are struggling, and advocating for better mental health services. Because at the end of the day, a **healthy mind is key to a healthy life**, and no amount of kale smoothies is going to fix that.

The Role of Clean Environments and Healthy Living in National Prosperity

Now, let's talk about something we all know but often forget: **a clean environment is the foundation of good health**. It's like the unsung hero of wellness. You can eat all the healthy food you want, exercise daily, and meditate like a monk, but if you're living in a polluted environment, you're fighting an uphill battle.

Here's the thing: **clean air, clean water, and clean surroundings** are not luxuries—they're basic necessities. Yet, we've somehow convinced ourselves that it's okay to live in environments where trash piles up on the streets, rivers look like something out of a dystopian movie, and air pollution is just a part of life. Newsflash: **it's not okay**. Dirty environments lead to all kinds of health problems, from respiratory diseases to waterborne illnesses, and they're dragging down our national prosperity faster than a corrupt tender deal.

But let's not get too down about it—because the good news is, we can fix this. It doesn't take a miracle; it just takes a little **effort from everyone**. First, let's stop throwing our trash everywhere like we're trying to mark our territory. Seriously, folks—there are bins for a reason. Second, let's support initiatives that clean up our rivers, streets, and public spaces. There are already plenty of community-driven environmental projects doing incredible work (shoutout to all the environmental warriors out there), but they need our help.

And let's not forget about **sustainable living**. It's not just a trend—it's the future. Whether it's reducing plastic use, conserving water, or planting trees, every small action counts. A **clean environment leads to a healthier population**, and a healthier population leads to a more productive, prosperous nation. It's like a domino effect, except in this version, the last domino is everyone being happy, healthy, and thriving.

Building Local Health Systems That Deliver Quality Care

Alright, now let's tackle the big one: **building local health systems that actually work**. Yes, I'm talking about hospitals that are fully stocked, clinics that don't turn people away, and health centers where the staff don't make you feel like you're bothering them just by existing.

We've all heard the horror stories. You go to a hospital, wait for hours (because apparently, time moves differently in medical facilities), only to be told that the medicine you need is "out of stock," or worse, that the doctor isn't available because he's on lunch break. Now, I'm not saying doctors shouldn't eat—everyone deserves lunch—but the whole system needs an overhaul if we're going to build a **culture of health and wellness**.

What we need are **local health systems** that are accessible, affordable, and provide **quality care**. That means making sure that every clinic, whether it's in the heart of Nairobi or a remote village in Turkana, has the resources it needs to provide essential services. It also means investing in **healthcare infrastructure**, training more medical professionals, and ensuring that healthcare workers are motivated and well-compensated. After all, no one's at their best when they're underpaid, overworked, and underappreciated.

We also need to start using **technology** to bridge the gap between urban and rural healthcare. Telemedicine, mobile clinics, and health apps can revolutionize the way we deliver care, especially in hard-to-reach areas. It's time to embrace innovation, because the future of healthcare isn't just in hospitals—it's in the palm of your hand.

Conclusion: Health Is the Real Wealth

So, what's the bottom line? **Health is wealth**, and if we don't take care of it, we're all going to be a lot poorer—both literally and figuratively. It's time to shift from a culture of reactive, crisis-mode healthcare to one of **preventive care**, where we take responsibility for our health before things go wrong. It's time to prioritize **mental health**, because a healthy mind is just as important as a healthy body. It's time to clean up our environment, because clean air and water are the foundation of a prosperous nation. And it's time to build **local health systems** that deliver quality care to every Kenyan, regardless of where they live.

The future of Kenya is bright, but only if we're healthy enough to enjoy it. So let's get serious about health and wellness—not because it's trendy, but because it's the only way we'll truly thrive as individuals and as a nation.

Now go out there, take care of yourself, and maybe—just maybe—skip the nyama choma this weekend. Your future self will thank you.

Empowering Women, Empowering Society – The Role of Gender Equality in National Progress

Ladies and gentlemen, gather around! It's time to talk about the unsung heroes of Kenya—the **women**. Yes, you heard me right. We're about to dive into a topic that's long overdue: **gender equality**. And before you sigh and think, "Here we go again with the feminist stuff," let me assure you, this is not going to be one of those lectures where we throw statistics at you like confetti. No, this is about the **real power of women**—and, spoiler alert: empowering women is not just about doing the right thing, it's about transforming **families, communities, and the nation** as a whole.

So buckle up, because we're about to explore how **gender equality** could very well be Kenya's secret weapon to unlocking a future filled with progress, prosperity, and, dare I say, peace. And we'll do it with a dash of humor, because who says gender equality can't be funny?

Shifting Cultural Perceptions of Gender Roles

Let's start by addressing the elephant in the room: **cultural perceptions of gender roles**. Now, in Kenya, as in many places, we have a somewhat... shall we say, **traditional view** of what men and women should do. Men are often expected to be the breadwinners, while women handle the home front—cooking, cleaning, raising the kids, and somehow managing to be everyone's personal therapist. It's like women are walking, talking Swiss Army knives, expected to do everything, and do it with a smile. And if that weren't enough, throw in some high heels, because apparently, looking fabulous is also part of the job description.

But here's the problem: these **old-school gender roles** are holding us back, big time. They limit the potential of half the population by making them believe that their place is in the kitchen (not that there's anything wrong with cooking, but let's be real—women belong **everywhere**). These outdated perceptions also place unnecessary pressure on men, who are expected to bear the weight of the world on their shoulders like they're auditioning to be the next Atlas.

The reality is, we need to **shift** how we see gender roles. Women can be, and already are, doing everything from running businesses to leading political movements, all while balancing family life. And men? Well, men can—and should—be involved in family life beyond just providing the finances. Imagine a world where **men and women share the load**, both at work and at home, where boys and girls grow up knowing they can pursue whatever dreams they want, regardless of their gender.

It's time to throw the old rulebook out the window, people. Gender roles? They're as outdated as a dial-up internet connection. Let's start seeing women as **partners in progress**, not just background players in the grand production of life. And let's give men the freedom to express themselves beyond the tired stereotype of the stoic provider. We'll all be happier for it.

How Empowering Women Improves Family, Community, and National Outcomes

Now, let's get down to the nitty-gritty: **empowering women doesn't just benefit women—it benefits everyone**. I know, shocking, right? When women are empowered, the whole country wins, and here's why.

1. Family Outcomes: Happy Wife, Happy Life

We've all heard the saying "happy wife, happy life," and while it may sound like something your uncle mutters after a long day, it's actually rooted in some truth. When women are empowered, families thrive. Studies show that when women have access to education, financial independence, and equal opportunities, they tend to invest back into their families—especially in their children's education and health.

When women have the ability to earn a decent income, their children are more likely to stay in school, get proper healthcare, and grow up with a better chance of breaking the cycle of poverty. So, when you empower a woman, you're essentially **empowering the next generation**, too. It's a win-win situation—kind of like getting extra fries with your meal without having to pay for them.

2. Community Outcomes: Women as Pillars of Society

When women are empowered at the community level, the entire community benefits. Take **women's self-help groups** as an example. In many rural areas across Kenya, women have come together to form savings and credit cooperatives, or "chamas," where they pool resources, support each other's businesses, and provide social and financial safety nets. These groups are the backbone of many rural economies, and they've allowed countless women to start businesses, pay for their children's education, and even invest in community infrastructure like water projects and schools.

What does this mean? It means that **empowered women are natural leaders** who build stronger, more resilient communities. They're the unsung heroes who keep everything running smoothly while managing to throw the best fundraisers the village has ever seen. Who wouldn't want that kind of leadership?

3. National Outcomes: The Economic Engine of Equality

Let's talk money for a second, because we all know that nothing grabs attention quite like the mention of **economic growth**. Here's the deal: when women participate fully in the economy, it's like adding rocket fuel to national development. Research shows that countries with higher levels of gender equality tend to have stronger economies. Why? Because when women work, they contribute to **economic productivity**, generate income, and create jobs.

Imagine if every woman in Kenya had the opportunity to pursue her career goals without barriers. The boost to the economy would be enormous. We're talking about increased GDP, reduced poverty, and a healthier, more dynamic labor force. Essentially, **empowering women is the best investment a country can make**. Forget fancy economic policies—just let women do their thing, and watch the country thrive.

Stories of Kenyan Women Breaking Barriers and Inspiring Change

Now, let's move on to my favorite part: the **stories of Kenyan women** who have broken barriers, smashed glass ceilings, and shown us all what's possible when women are empowered.

1. Wangari Maathai – Environmental Warrior

Let's start with the OG of women empowerment in
Kenya—**Wangari Maathai**. This woman wasn't just a
trailblazer; she was an **unstoppable force of nature** (pun
fully intended). In case you've been living under a rock,
Wangari Maathai was the founder of the **Green Belt
Movement**, an environmental conservation organization
that helped plant over 51 million trees across Kenya. She
was the first African woman to win the **Nobel Peace Prize**,
and she spent her life fighting for women's rights,
democracy, and environmental sustainability.

Wangari Maathai's story is one of resilience, courage, and
an unwavering commitment to doing what's right. She
faced opposition from all sides, but she never gave up. Her
legacy is proof that when women are empowered, they
don't just change their communities—they change the
world.

2. Tabitha Karanja – Entrepreneur Extraordinaire

Next up, we've got **Tabitha Karanja**, the woman who
dared to take on the beer industry and win. Tabitha is the
founder of **Keroche Breweries**, Kenya's first fully locally
owned beer and spirits manufacturer. In an industry
dominated by international giants, Tabitha built her
company from the ground up, despite facing numerous
challenges, including sexism and sabotage from
competitors.

Today, Keroche Breweries is a multi-billion-shilling
business, and Tabitha Karanja is an inspiration to women
entrepreneurs across the country. Her story shows that
women can succeed in any field—even those traditionally
dominated by men. All it takes is determination, vision, and

a little bit of fearlessness (and maybe a cold beer to celebrate afterward).

3. Phyllis Omido – The Voice of the Voiceless

Another incredible woman breaking barriers is **Phyllis Omido**, an environmental activist and community organizer. Known as the "East African Erin Brockovich," Phyllis fought tirelessly to shut down a lead-smelting factory in Mombasa that was poisoning the local community, including her own son. Despite threats to her life and constant pushback, Phyllis didn't back down. She founded the **Center for Justice, Governance, and Environmental Action**, and in 2015, she won the **Goldman Environmental Prize** for her work in environmental justice.

Phyllis Omido's story is a reminder that empowered women don't just stand up for themselves—they stand up for their communities. They fight for justice, even when the odds are stacked against them. And they win.

Legal and Cultural Reforms to Promote Gender Equality

Now, let's talk about what it will take to ensure that **gender equality isn't just a pipe dream** but a reality for every woman in Kenya. Because while we've made progress, there's still a long way to go.

1. Legal Reforms

First things first: we need **stronger legal protections for women's rights**. While Kenya's constitution guarantees gender equality, there are still significant gaps when it comes to the implementation of those laws. We need reforms that ensure equal pay for equal work, protect women from gender-based violence, and guarantee access to education, healthcare, and reproductive rights.

It's not enough to have laws on paper—they need to be enforced. This means training law enforcement, judiciary personnel, and public officials to take women's rights seriously. It also means creating safe spaces for women to report discrimination and abuse without fear of retaliation.

2. Cultural Reforms

Legal reforms are only half the battle. We also need to address the **deep-rooted cultural norms** that continue to hold women back. This means challenging the stereotypes that limit what women can do and shifting the narrative from one of submission to one of empowerment. Education is key here. We need to teach boys and girls from a young age that gender equality is non-negotiable. We need to show them examples of women leaders, entrepreneurs, and innovators so they grow up knowing that women can and should be in positions of power. And we need to engage men in the conversation because gender equality isn't a "women's issue"—it's an issue for all of us.

Conclusion: Empowering Women, Empowering Society

So, what's the takeaway? **Empowering women empowers society**. It's not just about giving women a seat at the table—it's about transforming the table itself. When women are empowered, families thrive, communities prosper, and the nation becomes stronger, more resilient, and more innovative.

Kenya has no shortage of inspiring women who are breaking barriers and leading the charge for change. But we need more than individual success stories. We need systemic change—both legal and cultural—to ensure that every woman in Kenya has the opportunity to reach her full potential.

The future of Kenya is female. And male. And everyone in between. It's a future where **gender equality** isn't just a goal—it's the norm. So let's roll up our sleeves, break down the barriers, and build a nation where every woman can rise, and when she rises, she lifts us all.

Innovation in Healthcare – From Traditional Medicine to Modern Healthcare Solutions

In Kenya, healthcare has always been a mix of tradition and innovation, like trying to blend goat stew with a side of high-tech medical devices. It's a place where centuries-old herbal remedies are used alongside the latest in mobile health apps, and where your grandma's concoction of boiled herbs might be recommended with the same enthusiasm as a doctor's prescription for antibiotics. The result is a fascinating, sometimes hilarious, and often deeply innovative healthcare landscape that reflects Kenya's unique ability to blend the old with the new.

For centuries, traditional medicine has played a central role in the lives of Kenyans. From the rolling hills of Kisii to the coastal villages of Mombasa, herbalists, bonesetters, and spiritual healers have provided care long before modern hospitals came onto the scene. And while modern healthcare has brought incredible advancements in medicine, surgery, and diagnostics, traditional medicine continues to hold its ground. The question now is: how do we integrate these two seemingly opposing systems to create a healthcare system that is accessible, effective, and affordable for all Kenyans?

In this chapter, we'll dive into the wild, wonderful, and occasionally laugh-out-loud funny world of healthcare innovation in Kenya. We'll explore how traditional medicine and modern healthcare are merging in unexpected ways, and how innovations like mobile health apps, telemedicine, and even "boda boda ambulances" are transforming healthcare access in both rural and urban areas. Along the way, we'll reflect on why your grandma's herbs might still be the best cure for the common cold— and how a simple text message could one day save your life.

Traditional Medicine: A Healing Heritage That Refuses to Go Away

Before there were doctors with stethoscopes and fancy medical degrees, there were herbalists with mortar and pestle, grinding roots and leaves into potions that could cure anything from stomachaches to evil spirits. In Kenya, traditional medicine has been passed down through generations, with every community having its own set of remedies for common ailments. Whether it's the Maasai using aloe vera to heal wounds or the Kikuyu brewing up a concoction made from tree bark to treat malaria, traditional medicine is a key part of the country's healthcare narrative.

For many Kenyans, traditional medicine isn't just an alternative to modern healthcare—it's the first line of defense. In rural areas where access to hospitals and clinics is limited, herbalists and traditional healers often serve as the local "doctors," trusted to diagnose illnesses, prescribe treatments, and even perform surgeries (although let's hope it's nothing too complicated). Traditional medicine is not just about herbs, though; it's also deeply rooted in spiritual beliefs, and healers often incorporate rituals and blessings to address the psychological and emotional aspects of illness.

One of the most hilarious—and sometimes frustrating—realities of traditional medicine in Kenya is that it often works side by side with modern healthcare, sometimes in unexpected ways. You'll hear stories of someone going to the hospital for a checkup, getting a diagnosis, and then heading straight to the local herbalist for "supplementary treatment." Got a headache? Sure, the doctor might prescribe painkillers, but your aunt will insist that a brew made from boiled pawpaw leaves is the real cure. It's like covering all your bases, but with more roots and less science.

Despite the skepticism that sometimes surrounds traditional medicine, there's no denying that it has played—and continues to play—a vital role in Kenya's healthcare system. In fact, the World Health Organization (WHO) estimates that around 80% of people in Africa still rely on traditional medicine for their primary healthcare needs. But with the rise of modern healthcare innovations, the question is no longer whether traditional medicine has a place in the healthcare system—it's how to integrate it effectively with modern medical practices.

The Best of Both Worlds: Merging Tradition with Modern Medicine

Enter the era of healthcare innovation, where traditional medicine and modern healthcare are no longer seen as competitors but as complementary systems that can work together to improve health outcomes. In recent years, there has been a growing recognition of the value that traditional medicine brings, particularly in areas where modern healthcare is not easily accessible. As a result, efforts are underway to merge the two systems in a way that benefits all Kenyans.

One of the most exciting developments in this area is the push to formally recognize and regulate traditional medicine. The **Kenya Medical Practitioners and Dentists Board (KMPDB)** has been working on creating a framework to integrate traditional medicine into the national healthcare system. This includes training traditional healers, standardizing practices, and ensuring that herbal treatments are safe and effective. Imagine your local herbalist, once operating out of a small hut in the

108

village, now wearing a lab coat and working alongside doctors at a rural health clinic. It's the ultimate fusion of the old and the new!

In some parts of Kenya, traditional healers are already working with modern healthcare professionals to improve patient care. For example, in certain rural areas, traditional birth attendants (TBAs) are being trained to work alongside midwives and doctors to provide safer childbirth experiences for mothers. These TBAs, who have been delivering babies for decades (and probably know more about childbirth than some newly graduated doctors), are now learning modern techniques like sterilization and emergency interventions. It's a win-win situation that ensures mothers get the best of both worlds: the cultural comfort of a traditional healer and the medical expertise of a trained professional.

But it's not just about integrating traditional healers into modern hospitals. There's also a growing interest in using traditional knowledge to develop new medicines. Researchers in Kenya are studying the medicinal properties of local plants to create modern pharmaceuticals. Imagine the day when a prescription for an antibiotic made from the leaves of an indigenous plant is printed out at your local pharmacy—it's not as far-fetched as you might think!

Healthcare on Two Wheels: Boda Boda Ambulances and Mobile Clinics

Of course, no discussion of healthcare innovation in Kenya would be complete without mentioning the incredibly creative (and often hilarious) solutions Kenyans have come up with to solve the problem of accessing medical care, particularly in rural areas. In a country where getting to the nearest hospital can sometimes involve crossing rivers, climbing mountains, or navigating dirt roads that turn into mudslides during the rainy season, transportation is a major challenge.

Enter the **boda boda ambulance**, an innovation that is equal parts practical and genius. In rural areas, where traditional ambulances can't always reach patients due to poor road conditions, boda bodas (motorcycle taxis) have been repurposed as makeshift ambulances. Equipped with stretchers, first-aid kits, and occasionally a driver with a sense of adventure, these boda boda ambulances have become a lifeline for people in remote areas who need urgent medical care.
The concept might sound a bit crazy—after all, the idea of someone being rushed to the hospital on the back of a motorcycle feels more like a scene from an action movie than a real healthcare solution—but it works. In areas like Siaya County and parts of Western Kenya, boda boda ambulances have significantly reduced maternal deaths by ensuring that pregnant women can reach health facilities in time for safe deliveries. It's not the smoothest ride, but when the alternative is walking for hours to the nearest clinic, a bumpy boda boda ride can feel like a blessing.

In addition to boda boda ambulances, mobile clinics are another innovative solution that's bringing healthcare to the people, instead of the other way around. These clinics— often housed in vans or trucks—travel to remote areas, offering services like vaccinations, HIV testing, and maternal health checkups. Some even come equipped with ultrasound machines, enabling pregnant women to get scans without ever setting foot in a hospital. It's healthcare on wheels, and while it might not be as fancy as a state-of-the-art hospital, it gets the job done.

Telemedicine: The Doctor Will See You... Via Zoom

As Kenya continues to embrace technology, one of the most transformative innovations in healthcare has been the rise of **telemedicine**. In a country where rural areas often struggle with a shortage of doctors, telemedicine has become a game-changer, allowing patients to consult with doctors and specialists without needing to travel long distances.

Imagine this: you're in a rural village in Turkana, and you've been feeling unwell for days. The nearest hospital is 100 kilometers away, and you don't have the money for transport. But instead of waiting for the symptoms to worsen, you simply walk into the local health clinic, where a nurse sets up a video call with a doctor in Nairobi. Within minutes, you're describing your symptoms to the doctor, who is able to diagnose your condition and send a prescription via text message to the nearest pharmacy. It's the future of healthcare, but it's happening right now.

Telemedicine platforms like **Baobab Circle, Daktari Online**, and **Access Afya** are leading the charge in bringing virtual healthcare to Kenya. These platforms allow patients to book online consultations, access medical advice, and even get referrals for further tests or treatment, all from the comfort of their homes. For people living in remote areas, telemedicine is a lifeline—especially during times of crisis, like the COVID-19 pandemic, when travel was restricted.

And let's not forget the added benefit of avoiding long queues at public hospitals (we've all been there—waiting in line for hours, only to be told that the doctor has gone for lunch). With telemedicine, healthcare is becoming more efficient, accessible, and—dare we say—convenient. Who knew that getting a check-up could be as easy as ordering pizza online?

The Mobile Health Revolution: Healthcare in the Palm of Your Hand

If you thought telemedicine was cool, wait until you hear about Kenya's mobile health (mHealth) revolution. In a country where almost everyone has a mobile phone (even if it's a feature phone held together with duct tape), mobile health apps are transforming how people access healthcare services.

One of the most popular mHealth apps in Kenya is **M-TIBA**, a mobile platform that allows users to save, send, and receive funds for healthcare. M-TIBA users can set aside money for future medical expenses and use their mobile wallets to pay for treatments at partner clinics and hospitals. It's like having health insurance, but without the paperwork or the monthly premiums. And best of all, it's accessible to people in low-income areas who might not otherwise have access to traditional insurance schemes.

Other mHealth apps, like **MyDawa** and **TotoHealth**, are helping Kenyans manage everything from chronic diseases to maternal health. MyDawa, for example, allows users to purchase prescription medications online and have them delivered to their homes. TotoHealth, on the other hand, sends weekly text messages to pregnant women and new mothers, providing health tips and reminders for checkups and vaccinations. It's healthcare in the palm of your hand, and it's changing the way people think about medical care.

Of course, like any good Kenyan innovation, mHealth comes with its own set of challenges—mostly in the form of hilariously confused elderly relatives trying to figure out how to use the apps. If you've ever tried to teach your grandmother how to send an M-Pesa, you know exactly what we mean. But once people get the hang of it, the benefits are undeniable. With mHealth, healthcare is becoming more personalized, more accessible, and—most importantly—more affordable for all Kenyans.

Conclusion: The Future of Healthcare in Kenya

Kenya's healthcare system is a blend of tradition, innovation, and good old-fashioned Kenyan creativity. From traditional medicine to telemedicine, from boda boda ambulances to mobile health apps, the country is proving that you don't need a billion-dollar healthcare budget to come up with solutions that work. What you do need is a willingness to think outside the box, to embrace both the old and the new, and to keep an open mind about what "healthcare" really means.

As Kenya continues to develop its healthcare system, the integration of traditional medicine and modern innovations will be key to creating a system that serves everyone. Whether it's through training traditional healers, expanding telemedicine, or building more mobile clinics, the future of healthcare in Kenya looks bright—and, as always, full of surprises.

So, here's to the doctors, herbalists, boda boda riders, tech innovators, and everyday Kenyans who are working together to make healthcare more inclusive, accessible, and effective. Whether you're curing a headache with pawpaw leaves or booking a doctor's appointment via Zoom, one thing is clear: Kenya's healthcare system is a world of innovation and creativity like no other. And if you ever find yourself in need of a cure, just remember—you can always trust your grandma's advice, but it doesn't hurt to get a second opinion from the local clinic, too.

Youth as the Engine of Change – Empowering the Next Generation

If you want to witness the raw, unstoppable force that is Kenya's youth, just visit any matatu stage (bus stop) in Nairobi during rush hour. There you'll find young Kenyans hustling with the determination of a marathon runner and the creativity of a street artist. From hawking the latest knockoff sneakers to directing traffic with the precision of a military general, Kenya's youth are everywhere, finding innovative ways to navigate the chaos of everyday life. It's like watching a live-action TED Talk, except with more energy drinks and a bit of organized chaos.

But while Kenya's youth may be navigating the city streets with swagger, they're also navigating something much more important: the future of the country. With over 75% of the population under the age of 35, Kenya is a young country. This youthful energy holds the potential to drive change, fuel innovation, and push the country into new heights of progress. But here's the catch—tapping into this potential is like trying to herd a million caffeinated goats across a busy highway. If done right, the rewards are enormous. If not, well… let's just say things could get messy.

In this chapter, we'll explore the power of youth in Kenya and why empowering the next generation is the key to building a brighter, more dynamic future. From leadership to entrepreneurship to innovation, young Kenyans are already leading the way in many sectors, but they need more opportunities, more platforms, and a whole lot more support. So, buckle up, grab your smartphone (because you know the youth can't function without one), and get ready to dive into the hilarious, inspiring, and sometimes chaotic world of Kenyan youth.

The Youthquake: When Generation Z Meets Old-School Leadership

Kenya's leadership is like that stubborn grandfather who refuses to give up the remote control during family gatherings, despite the fact that no one wants to watch *"Machachari"* reruns for the millionth time. The youth, on the other hand, are like that one cousin who's quietly setting up Netflix on their phone in the corner, ready to stream something new, exciting, and relevant. Therein lies the problem: the country's leadership is still largely in the hands of the old guard, while the youth are chomping at the bit, ready to take over.

And make no mistake, Kenya's young people are not content to sit back and wait for their turn. They're demanding a seat at the table, or if necessary, they're building their own table. Whether it's through social media activism, entrepreneurship, or community organizing, Kenya's youth are finding creative ways to influence policy and drive progress—even if they have to shake things up to get noticed.

Take the rise of youth-led political movements, for example. In recent years, we've seen young Kenyans step up and challenge the status quo, refusing to be sidelined in decisions that affect their future. From organizing voter registration drives to running for office themselves, young people are making it clear that they are not just the leaders of tomorrow—they're the leaders of today. Sure, there are a few raised eyebrows from the old-school politicians who are still trying to figure out how to use Twitter, but the message is clear: the youth are here, and they're not going anywhere.

The challenge, of course, is bridging the gap between Kenya's traditional leadership structures and the fresh, bold ideas of the younger generation. It's like trying to mix sukuma wiki (collard greens) with pizza—both are delicious in their own right, but getting them to work together might require a bit of experimentation. But with the right mentorship, platforms, and opportunities, there's no doubt that Kenya's youth can and will lead the country into the future.

Entrepreneurs-in-Chief: Hustling, Innovating, and Taking Over

If there's one thing Kenya's youth know how to do, it's hustle. Whether it's selling boiled eggs on the side of the road or developing the next big app in a tech hub, young Kenyans have entrepreneurship running through their veins. And it's not just about survival—it's about innovation, creativity, and turning obstacles into opportunities.

Consider Kenya's booming tech industry, often referred to as "Silicon Savannah." This tech revolution is being driven largely by young innovators who are finding creative solutions to everyday problems. From mobile banking apps like M-Pesa to agricultural platforms that help farmers get real-time market prices, young Kenyans are leveraging technology to transform industries. And let's not forget the wave of fintech startups, where young entrepreneurs are redefining how people access financial services in a country where traditional banking can feel like an Olympic sport.

But the hustle doesn't stop at tech. Kenya's youth are making waves in agriculture, fashion, arts, and even

environmental conservation. Take the "agripreneurs"—
young Kenyans who are turning farming into a profitable,
tech-savvy business. Gone are the days when agriculture
was seen as something for rural folks and retirees. Today,
young Kenyans are using drones to monitor crops,
blockchain to track produce, and social media to sell fresh
vegetables straight from the farm to your doorstep. It's
farming, but with Wi-Fi and a side of avocado toast.

Still, entrepreneurship in Kenya comes with its own set of
challenges. Access to capital remains a major hurdle,
especially for young people who don't have the
connections or financial backing to get their ideas off the
ground. The good news? Kenya's youth are nothing if not
resourceful. With crowdfunding, mobile banking platforms,
and government initiatives like the Youth Enterprise
Development Fund, young entrepreneurs are finding ways
to fund their dreams. And when all else fails, there's always
the "mshwari" loan—a quick mobile loan that, while high
in interest, has been known to save a business or two in a
pinch.

Social Media: The Youth's Political Platform and Meme Playground

When it comes to influencing policy and driving progress,
Kenyan youth have found a new weapon of choice: social
media. If the older generation is still writing long letters to
the editor in the newspaper, the youth are busy crafting
280-character takedowns on Twitter, posting meme-filled
manifestos on Instagram, and starting viral campaigns on
TikTok.

Social media isn't just a tool for sharing cat videos
(although Kenyan Twitter is full of them)—it's become a

powerful platform for youth-led activism. From #MyDressMyChoice, which brought attention to the harassment of women, to #JusticeForKhadija, which demanded justice for gender-based violence victims, social media is where the youth are organizing, advocating, and holding the government accountable. The best part? They're doing it with a sense of humor that can't be matched.

Take #KOT (Kenyans on Twitter), for example—a collective of online warriors who can turn a serious political issue into a trending topic faster than you can say *"Wanjiru for President."* KOT has gained a reputation for being witty, sharp-tongued, and fearless, taking on everyone from corrupt politicians to big corporations. It's grassroots activism, but with a dash of meme culture and a side of sarcasm. And the politicians? Well, some of them are trying to keep up, but let's just say their social media game is about as smooth as a matatu ride on a pothole-filled road.

But social media is more than just a playground for political memes—it's also a space where young Kenyans are shaping the national conversation. Whether it's discussing climate change, economic policies, or mental health, social media gives youth a voice in a country where traditional political spaces have often been dominated by the older generation. It's democratic, it's inclusive, and—best of all—it's free. Well, except for the cost of data bundles, but even that can be negotiated when the hustle is real.

Education and Innovation: Unlocking the Next Big Thing

While Kenya's youth are already making waves in leadership and entrepreneurship, one of the biggest keys to unlocking their full potential is education. But we're not just talking about the traditional "sit down and memorize" education that makes you feel like you've been sent to detention for 12 years. We're talking about education that sparks creativity, encourages problem-solving, and prepares young people for the future.

Unfortunately, Kenya's education system hasn't always kept up with the times. While it's produced plenty of brilliant minds, it's also been known to emphasize rote learning over critical thinking. That's where innovation comes in. Schools and universities are starting to recognize the importance of nurturing talent in technology, the arts, and entrepreneurship. Programs like the Presidential Digital Talent Programme are training the next generation of tech experts, while initiatives like AkiraChix are empowering young women to become tech innovators in a traditionally male-dominated field.

The goal is to equip young Kenyans with the skills they need to thrive in a rapidly changing world—whether that's through coding boot camps, creative arts workshops, or vocational training programs that prepare them for the jobs of tomorrow. And while there's still a long way to go in making education accessible to all, the shift toward innovation-driven learning is a sign that Kenya's youth are being prepared for more than just passing exams—they're being prepared to change the world.

The Youth Economy: Jobs, Jobs, and More Jobs (Or Lack Thereof)

Of course, it's hard to talk about youth empowerment without addressing the elephant in the room: jobs. Kenya's youth face an unemployment rate of nearly 40%, and while the entrepreneurial spirit is alive and well, not everyone wants to or can start their own business. The reality is that there simply aren't enough jobs to go around, and those that do exist often require the infamous "5 years of experience" that no recent graduate can seem to find.

So what's the solution? The answer lies in creating pathways to employment that reflect the realities of the modern workforce. That means investing in industries that have the potential to create jobs on a large scale, such as technology, manufacturing, and agriculture. It also means encouraging apprenticeship programs, internships, and mentorship opportunities that allow young people to gain practical skills while still in school. In an ideal world, every university graduate would step right into a job that perfectly matches their skills and passion—but this is Kenya, so we have to be a bit more creative.

The government has rolled out programs like the **Kazi Mtaani** initiative, which aims to provide temporary jobs for youth in urban areas by involving them in community projects like street cleaning and road maintenance. While it's a step in the right direction, temporary jobs alone won't solve the long-term unemployment crisis. What's needed is a deeper commitment to creating sustainable employment opportunities that tap into the potential of young people.

And let's not forget the private sector, which plays a crucial role in providing jobs for Kenya's youth. Companies, both local and multinational, are beginning to recognize the value of hiring young, innovative minds. After all, young people bring fresh perspectives, tech-savviness, and boundless energy to the workplace. The challenge is to create an environment where young employees can thrive and grow, not just be treated as interns fetching coffee.

The Future Is Youth: Leading the Charge for a Better Kenya

Kenya's youth are not just the future—they're the present. They're hustling, innovating, leading, and making their voices heard in every corner of the country. Whether it's through entrepreneurship, social media activism, or community leadership, young Kenyans are driving progress in ways that are bold, dynamic, and often hilarious.

But for Kenya to truly harness the power of its youth, more needs to be done. It's about creating pathways for young people to participate in leadership, providing the tools they need to succeed as entrepreneurs, and equipping them with the skills that the future demands. It's about investing in education that sparks innovation and nurturing the talents that will lead the country into the next phase of development. Most importantly, it's about recognizing that Kenya's youth are not a problem to be solved—they're the solution.

So, to all the young people out there—whether you're leading a movement, launching a startup, or just trying to navigate the complexities of everyday life—know this: you are the engine of change. You are the force that will push Kenya forward. And as you continue to innovate, hustle, and lead, you're not just changing your future—you're changing the future of Kenya itself.

In conclusion, empowering Kenya's youth is not just an option; it's a necessity. They are the heartbeat of the nation, the unstoppable force that can drive progress in ways we can only imagine. With the right support, guidance, and opportunities, there's no limit to what young Kenyans can achieve. As the saying goes, *"The future belongs to the young."* In Kenya's case, the future is already here, and it's wearing a snapback, sipping on a cold soda, and tweeting about the next big idea. Watch out, world—Kenya's youth are coming for you, and they're bringing the change we've all been waiting for.

KEYPOINTS AND SUMMARY

Education as Social Mobility: Education lifts people out of poverty, creating opportunities for national progress.

Lifelong Learning: Education is continuous, essential for staying relevant, and vocational skills are crucial for economic development.

Urban-Rural Gap: Bridging the divide requires better infrastructure, teacher training, and technological solutions to ensure equitable education.

Innovative Initiatives: Programs like the M-Pesa Foundation Academy, Bridge International Academies, and AkiraChix are driving educational transformation by offering affordable, quality education and empowering marginalized communities.

Future of Education: Investing in education is key to Kenya's success, offering a brighter future for all.

Health is Wealth: Emphasizes the importance of health, often neglected until crisis strikes.

Preventive Healthcare: Calls for a shift from reactive care to preventive measures like regular check-ups, healthy living, and vaccinations.

Mental Health: Advocates for breaking the stigma around mental health, promoting awareness, and creating support systems.

Clean Environment: Highlights the role of clean air, water, and surroundings in promoting good health and national prosperity.

Local Health Systems: Urges investment in accessible, affordable, and efficient healthcare, especially in rural areas, with a focus on technology-driven solutions.

Cultural Gender Perceptions: Traditional gender roles limit women's potential and place unnecessary pressure on men. Shifting these perceptions is key to progress.

Family Impact: Empowering women improves family outcomes, particularly in education and health.
Community Impact: Women in leadership roles, like in self-help groups, strengthen communities.
National Impact: Gender equality boosts economic growth; women's participation in the economy drives national prosperity.
Inspiring Women: Wangari Maathai, Tabitha Karanja, and Phyllis Omido show how empowered women transform society.
Needed Reforms: Legal reforms to protect women's rights and cultural shifts challenging stereotypes are essential for gender equality.

Healthcare in Kenya: A blend of traditional remedies and modern medical innovations.
Traditional Medicine: Continues to play a key role in rural areas where access to modern healthcare is limited.
Integration of Systems: Efforts to merge traditional practices with modern healthcare through regulation and training.
Innovations: Creative solutions like boda boda ambulances and mobile clinics enhance access to healthcare.
Telemedicine: Virtual consultations improve healthcare delivery, especially in remote areas.
mHealth Apps: Platforms like M-TIBA and MyDawa make healthcare services more accessible and affordable.
Future Outlook: Combining tradition and innovation to create an inclusive healthcare system.

Kenya's Youth: Represent over 75% of the population and are vital to the nation's future.
Entrepreneurial Spirit: Youth are leading innovation in tech, agriculture, and business, but face challenges like limited access to capital.

Youth Political Engagement: Young Kenyans are pushing for leadership roles and policy influence, often using social media activism.

Education and Innovation: Kenya's education system is evolving to foster creativity and problem-solving.

Youth Unemployment: High unemployment rates call for sustainable job creation in key sectors.

Empowering the Future: Youth are driving progress and need more opportunities and support to lead Kenya forward.

Entrepreneurs as Game Changers – Unlocking Innovation and Self-Reliance

Picture this: A young man in Kenya graduates from university, clutching his degree like it's a golden ticket to success. He's beaming, full of hope, and has already started dreaming about his first office job in the bustling city, complete with a tie, shiny shoes, and a snazzy briefcase. He can already imagine himself sitting at a desk, sipping coffee while giving PowerPoint presentations about "synergy" and "increasing ROI." Little does he know, reality is about to slap him in the face harder than a hot ugali on a cold plate.

He starts job hunting. Weeks turn into months, months into years. He attends interviews that go nowhere, submits CVs that seem to vanish into the abyss of forgotten documents, and hears the dreaded phrase, "We'll get back to you," so many times it haunts him in his sleep. The job market, my friends, is tighter than a pair of jeans after Christmas. And this young man, like millions of other Kenyans, is stuck in the frustrating cycle of job-seeking with no job in sight.

But wait! Enter entrepreneurship—the shining beacon of hope, the underdog of economic growth, the superpower that can turn this jobless struggle into a story of triumph. Entrepreneurship isn't just an option anymore; it's the game changer we need to unlock innovation and self-reliance. Let's dive into how shifting from job-seeking to job creation can transform Kenya into a hub of innovation, development, and maybe even a little humor along the way.

Shifting from Job-Seeking to Job Creation

First things first: **Kenya's job market is as overworked and overcrowded as a Nairobi matatu at rush hour.** Everyone's in a rush to get somewhere, but it feels like we're all stuck in traffic, honking at each other, and hoping the guy in front of us doesn't suddenly hit the brakes. It's a mess, and we need a way out.

Now, traditionally, the goal was always to get a "good job." You know, the kind that makes your parents brag about you at church, the kind that makes your relatives ask, "So, are you planning on buying land soon?" But let's face it—those jobs are becoming rarer than a politician who keeps their promises. With an exploding population, limited formal jobs, and technological disruptions shaking things up faster than a boda boda on a rough road, job-seeking just isn't what it used to be.

And here's where the magic happens: **entrepreneurship.** Instead of waiting for someone to give you a job, why not create one? Better yet, why not create jobs for others? It's time to embrace the entrepreneurial mindset, where every problem is an opportunity, and every challenge is a chance to innovate.

Imagine if, instead of searching for a job, our fresh graduate decides to open a small business. Maybe he starts a coffee shop where customers can work, socialize, and drink the kind of coffee that doesn't taste like hot water with a hint of sadness. Or maybe he gets into agribusiness, turning that dusty plot of land his family owns into a thriving vegetable farm. The possibilities are endless! And guess what? When he succeeds, he's not just helping himself; he's employing others, boosting the local economy, and maybe—just maybe—paying enough taxes to fund those elusive pothole repairs we've all been dreaming about.

How Entrepreneurship Can Drive National Development

Now, if you're still skeptical about entrepreneurship as the ultimate game changer, let's look at how it **drives national development.**

Job Creation:

> When entrepreneurs succeed, they create jobs—not just for themselves, but for others too. This is especially important in Kenya, where youth unemployment is through the roof. Every time someone opens a small business, hires an assistant, or expands their operations, that's one less person waiting in line at the job center.

Innovation:

> Entrepreneurs are natural problem solvers. They look at the world and see gaps that need filling, problems that need fixing, and opportunities that others miss. Whether it's finding new ways to deliver goods and services or developing tech solutions that make life easier (seriously, have you tried sending money with M-Pesa lately? It's like magic), entrepreneurs push the boundaries of what's possible.

Boosting the Economy:

> Entrepreneurs don't just sit around waiting for the economy to grow—they make it grow. Every time someone buys from a small business, money flows back into the economy. That coffee shop owner? He's buying beans from local farmers. The farmer?

He's buying tools from a local supplier. It's a cycle of economic goodness that lifts everyone up.

Reducing Poverty:

When people have jobs, they can afford to feed their families, educate their children, and invest in their futures. Entrepreneurship plays a key role in reducing poverty because it empowers individuals to take control of their own economic destinies. Plus, when small businesses grow, they often contribute to local development projects, like building schools or supporting health initiatives. So, yeah—entrepreneurs are basically superheroes in disguise.

Building a Culture of Innovation and Adaptability

If entrepreneurship is the answer, then we need to build a culture that embraces **innovation and adaptability**—two words that should be as common in our conversations as "corruption" and "traffic jams" (but, you know, in a positive way).

The problem is that many people still view entrepreneurship as risky, unstable, or only for the "lucky few" who manage to make it big. But here's the truth: **innovation isn't just for Silicon Valley tech moguls or genius inventors** who start businesses in their garages. Innovation is for everyone—whether you're selling vegetables in Gikomba Market, developing the next app, or running a roadside kiosk that serves the best samosas in town.

Adaptability is key here. The world is changing fast, and the only way to survive is to change with it. Entrepreneurs are like the chameleons of the business world—constantly adapting to new challenges, new markets, and new ways of doing things. Just look at how businesses pivoted during the COVID-19 pandemic—those who adapted to online delivery or digital platforms thrived, while others were left scratching their heads, wondering what just happened.
To build a culture of innovation and adaptability, we need to:

Encourage risk-taking: Failure is not the end of the world, folks. In fact, it's often the beginning of something great. Entrepreneurs need to embrace failure as a learning experience and not a death sentence. As they say, if at first you don't succeed, try again—or in the case of Kenyan entrepreneurs, maybe try a different business altogether.

Promote creativity: Every great business idea starts with creativity. Whether it's figuring out how to deliver goods more efficiently, coming up with new flavors for your chapati business, or inventing an app that makes paying bills less painful, creativity is the secret sauce that keeps entrepreneurs ahead of the curve.

Foster collaboration: Entrepreneurship doesn't have to be a solo mission. Some of the best businesses come from partnerships and collaborations. Think about it—Steve Jobs had Steve Wozniak, Bill Gates had Paul Allen, and, well, Batman had Robin. Okay, maybe not the last one, but you get the point. Working together allows entrepreneurs to pool their resources, share ideas, and tackle bigger challenges.

Support entrepreneurship from a young age: We need to teach entrepreneurship in schools, not just as a career option but as a mindset. Imagine if students learned to see problems as opportunities and were encouraged to come up with innovative solutions from a young age. Instead of being told, "Get good grades so you can get a job," they'd be told, "Get good grades so you can change the world." How's that for inspiring?

Lessons from Successful Kenyan Entrepreneurs

And now, for the moment you've all been waiting for— **real-life success stories** of Kenyan entrepreneurs who've made it big through innovation, hard work, and a healthy dose of determination. If these stories don't inspire you to start your own business, I don't know what will.

1. Mike Macharia – Seven Seas Technologies
Let's start with **Mike Macharia**, the founder and CEO of **Seven Seas Technologies**, one of the leading IT companies in East Africa. Mike didn't just stumble upon success—he built it from the ground up. At just 25 years old, he started his company with a laptop, a dream, and the belief that IT could transform industries in Kenya. Fast forward a few years, and Seven Seas Technologies is now providing cutting-edge IT solutions for healthcare, finance, and government sectors across Africa.

Mike's journey teaches us that **you don't need to be a genius with a fancy degree** to make it big. What you need is vision, persistence, and the willingness to take risks. Today, Seven Seas Technologies is not only successful but is also helping to revolutionize industries and create jobs.

2. Tabitha Karanja – Keroche Breweries

Next, we have **Tabitha Karanja**, the founder of **Keroche Breweries**, a homegrown Kenyan company that dared to take on the giants of the alcohol industry. When she started her business in the 1990s, the beer market in Kenya was dominated by one major player—so naturally, everyone thought she was crazy. But Tabitha wasn't intimidated. She believed in her product, fought through countless obstacles, and today, **Keroche Breweries** is a multi-million-dollar company that's giving the big boys a run for their money.

What can we learn from Tabitha? First, **never let anyone tell you it can't be done**—especially if you're a woman in a male-dominated industry. Second, **believe in your product**, and third, **never back down** from a challenge. Her entrepreneurial journey is a masterclass in resilience, determination, and innovation.

3. Peter Njonjo – Twiga Foods

Finally, meet **Peter Njonjo**, the co-founder of **Twiga Foods**, a company that's transforming Kenya's agricultural sector. Twiga Foods connects smallholder farmers to vendors, reducing food waste, cutting out middlemen, and ensuring that fresh produce gets from farms to tables faster than ever before. It's like Uber, but for bananas—and tomatoes, and onions, and everything else you find at the market.

Peter's story shows us the power of using technology to solve real-world problems. Twiga Foods isn't just a business—it's a solution to the inefficiencies that have plagued Kenya's agricultural supply chains for decades. By using **innovation and technology**, Peter is helping to ensure that farmers get a fair price for their produce, vendors get fresh supplies, and consumers get better quality food.

The Future is Bright for Kenyan Entrepreneurs

So, where do we go from here? The answer is simple: **entrepreneurship is the future**. It's the engine that will drive Kenya's development, create jobs, and unlock the innovation we need to thrive in a fast-changing world. Whether you're starting a tech company, opening a roadside kiosk, or inventing the next big thing in agriculture, entrepreneurship is the key to unlocking your potential—and Kenya's.

It's time to stop waiting for that elusive job and start creating one. It's time to embrace failure as part of the journey, to innovate, adapt, and collaborate. And most importantly, it's time to believe that you can make a difference.

After all, if the chameleon can change colors to survive, so can you.

The future belongs to the bold, the creative, and the entrepreneurial. So go out there, start something, and maybe—just maybe—you'll be the next Mike Macharia, Tabitha Karanja, or Peter Njonjo. **Kenya's future is in your hands, and it's time to make it happen.**

Technology and the Digital Revolution –
Preparing Kenya for the Future

Picture this: it's a bright, bustling Nairobi morning in 2024, and a man is standing in a long, winding queue at a government office. He's holding a paper form the size of a small tablecloth, his ID card from 1978, and his patience is hanging on by a thread thinner than a Safaricom signal in a basement. As he shifts his weight, staring blankly at a flickering fluorescent light above, his phone buzzes. The latest tweet from the Ministry of Technology reads: *"Kenya is on the verge of a digital revolution!"* A single tear rolls down his cheek.

Welcome to the great paradox that is Kenya's digital revolution. It's a world where we're busy talking about blockchain while still dodging potholes the size of swimming pools, and where the idea of e-government often feels like an elaborate prank. But hold on—Kenya *is* on the cusp of something spectacular, and the digital future is much closer than most of us think. This chapter is about that journey, from the daily battles with tech to the dreams of Kenya emerging as a shining beacon of technological innovation on the continent.

The (Mis)Adventures in Digital Literacy

Let's start with the basics: digital literacy. It's like learning to ride a bike, except the bike is made of algorithms, the pedals are social media apps, and the road is paved with memes. In Kenya, the digital journey begins with WhatsApp groups—those vast, noisy corners of the internet where everyone's aunt is the admin. From organizing wedding contributions to announcing village meetings, WhatsApp is the undisputed king of Kenyan communication. It's efficient, sure, but the downside? The dreaded family group where fake news spreads faster than a matatu on Mombasa Road.

Take, for example, Uncle Maina, who once forwarded a chain message to the entire family group warning that "if you don't forward this to 10 people, your phone will catch fire." Of course, he did this right after sending a picture of a goat claiming it was his "spirit animal." Uncle Maina's learning curve with technology has been steep, but he's not alone. Many Kenyans are still grappling with the idea of what it means to be "digital." It's not just about owning a smartphone, it's about knowing how to use it effectively without trying to take selfies with the screen facing away from you.

But that's just the start. Digital literacy in Kenya is growing rapidly, and with it, we're seeing an incredible wave of young tech-savvy Kenyans who are more comfortable coding in Python than frying an egg. The rise of coding boot camps, online courses, and tech hubs across the country is creating a new breed of problem solvers who are more likely to build an app to order mandazi than walk to the kiosk. This is the future—one where technology is not just a tool, but a way of life.

From "Please Restart" to "We Can Code That"

The most common phrase uttered by tech support in Kenya? "Have you tried turning it off and on again?" It's almost a national anthem for those struggling with technology. But in Kenya's new tech-savvy world, we're moving beyond simple troubleshooting. We're now talking about coding, automation, and artificial intelligence (AI). That's right: AI. Not to be confused with "Auntie Irene," who believes she's already the family's most intelligent being after downloading two news apps.

Kenya is transforming from a nation that once saw technology as a luxury to one that's becoming a serious player in the global tech scene. The rise of innovation hubs like iHub and Gearbox is creating spaces where young minds can build the next M-Pesa (which, let's face it, has already revolutionized how we view money). Kenya's Silicon Savannah is no longer a pipe dream. It's happening. Young tech entrepreneurs are creating apps that solve everything from finding directions to the nearest boda boda (motorbike taxi) to farming solutions that would make Jomo Kenyatta proud.

Take the case of "NyanyaTech," a fictional but totally plausible app that connects you directly to farmers for fresh produce delivery. You're scrolling through your phone at 10 p.m., craving some sukuma wiki (collard greens). NyanyaTech guarantees next-day delivery. You're set. Now, does the app also manage to deliver hilarious conversations with the farmer about how the greens are *very organic, no chemicals, and a little sunshine from Meru"*? Yes. This is innovation Kenyan-style—personal, local, and often with a side of humor.

Governance in the Digital Age: "Eh, Serikali Yako Iko App?"

Now, let's talk about governance and the digital revolution. For decades, interacting with the Kenyan government has been an experience best described as *"character-building."* You'd leave your house at dawn, armed with every form of identification known to man, only to find that the person who processes the paperwork "will return after tea break," which could be any time between 10 a.m. and Judgment Day.

Enter e-government, the digital solution to all our bureaucratic woes—or at least that's the dream. The Kenyan government has taken strides to digitize processes, and some services can now be accessed with just a few clicks. Need to renew your driver's license? No problem—log onto the NTSA portal, and you're good to go. That is, of course, if the website isn't down for maintenance, and your Wi-Fi doesn't decide to take an extended lunch break.

While we're not quite there yet, the future holds exciting potential. Imagine a Kenya where all government services are digitized, where you can pay your taxes, renew your passport, and lodge a complaint about your neighbor's noisy rooster without leaving your living room. It's coming, and when it does, Kenyans will likely reminisce about the days when we spent half our lives queuing at Huduma Centres (service centers). Maybe we'll even miss it. But probably not.

Education and the Digital Classroom: "Si You Google?"

In the world of education, Kenya is experiencing a quiet revolution. Gone are the days when students relied solely on textbooks, some of which were last updated when dinosaurs roamed the earth. Now, classrooms across the country are becoming digitized, with access to online resources, e-learning platforms, and digital classrooms.

Let's not kid ourselves—students still use Google for "research" in ways that would make their teachers cry. If you're a Kenyan student and haven't tried googling "How to pass exams without studying," are you even Kenyan? But beyond the memes and shortcuts, digital education is empowering students to learn at their own pace, access global knowledge, and develop skills that are increasingly necessary in a tech-driven world.

We now have coding as part of the curriculum in some schools, and initiatives like the "Digital Literacy Program" are providing devices to young learners. The vision? A Kenya where the next Steve Jobs is born in Kisumu, and the next Sheryl Sandberg hails from Machakos. And while we're still figuring out how to balance screen time with actual learning (yes, Netflix is *not* a study tool), the future looks incredibly bright.

Kenya as Africa's Tech Hub: "The Silicon Savannah"

Kenya's status as the Silicon Savannah is not just a catchy slogan. It's becoming a reality. M-Pesa set the stage, and now, a wave of homegrown innovations is poised to take Africa, and the world, by storm. Kenyan startups are receiving international recognition, attracting investments, and creating jobs that are reshaping the economy.

One minute you're discussing the potential of a "cashless society" in Nairobi, the next you're in a matatu (public minibus) listening to a driver demand "cash only" because "he doesn't trust those apps." We're living in a time of incredible change, where tradition and innovation coexist, sometimes awkwardly, but always with a sense of hope and humor.

The dream of Kenya as Africa's tech hub is within reach, but it requires more than just clever apps. It will take government support, investment in infrastructure, and a concerted effort to ensure that all Kenyans, from Nairobi to Mandera, have access to the tools of the digital age. We'll need to move beyond the "restart the router" mindset and into a future where tech is used to solve real problems, drive economic growth, and create a better quality of life for everyone.

The Laughs Ahead: Tech Fails and Future Wins

Of course, no journey into the digital future is without its bumps. Expect plenty of hilarious tech fails along the way. Wi-Fi that disappears just when you need it most, emails that vanish into the void, and apps that update at the worst possible moment. But that's all part of the fun. Kenya's tech revolution will be one filled with laughter, innovation, and an unbreakable spirit.

In the end, Kenya's digital revolution is about more than just gadgets and apps. It's about people. It's about a country ready to leap into the future, one laugh, one tech fail, and one innovation at a time. And that future? It's going to be bright, connected, and absolutely hilarious.

Infrastructure for Growth – Connecting Kenya to Opportunities

Let's begin with a scenario every Kenyan can relate to: You're seated in a matatu (public minibus), somewhere along the Thika Superhighway. The engine has overheated for the third time in an hour. The driver, now more of a comedian than a professional chauffeur, steps out and starts pouring what appears to be holy water on the radiator while muttering something about road blessings. Meanwhile, on your phone, the 4G signal is fluctuating between non-existent and "Please turn on airplane mode." You sigh and mutter under your breath, *"If only this infrastructure worked..."*

Welcome to Kenya—a land where infrastructure is the ultimate comedy show, starring potholes so large they have their own postal codes and Wi-Fi connections that seem to operate on a different calendar. Despite the chaos, infrastructure development is the key to unlocking Kenya's future. It's the thread that connects villages to cities, ideas to markets, and people to opportunities. If we get it right, Kenya could transform into a continental powerhouse. If we don't? Well, we'll be watching more drivers throw water on overheated engines while we wrestle with buffering YouTube videos.

Let's take a hilarious yet hopeful dive into Kenya's infrastructure situation, from roads that seem allergic to rain, to broadband speeds that would make a tortoise proud, and everything in between. Spoiler alert: this story involves both laughter and optimism, because even if our roads are bumpy, our spirit is unshakable.

The Road to Nowhere (And Everywhere)

They say all roads lead to Rome, but in Kenya, all roads seem to lead to traffic jams. Forget ancient European routes, we've got highways that start as smooth as a baby's bottom and then suddenly transform into lunar landscapes.

Whether you're driving to Kisumu, Eldoret, or Mombasa, you're likely to encounter potholes the size of small ponds. It's a rite of passage.

Take the Great Kenyan Road Trip, for example. You start your journey filled with hope, zipping along in your well-maintained Toyota, and somewhere between Naivasha and Nakuru, you hit the first pothole. At this point, you don't worry—you simply mutter, *"Eh, si they'll fix it one day."* Five hours later, after dodging craters like an Olympic hurdler, you've decided that Kenya's roads are best navigated with a 4x4 or a helicopter.

But here's the thing: despite the humor in our bumpy rides, roads are the lifeblood of any economy. Kenya's road network, as haphazard as it sometimes seems, is expanding and connecting parts of the country that were once inaccessible. The Thika Superhighway, despite its eternal traffic jams, is a marvel in terms of connecting Nairobi to the industrial areas of Thika and beyond. Roads like the Lamu Port-South Sudan-Ethiopia-Transport (LAPSSET) corridor project are ambitious and hold the promise of transforming regional trade.

However, there's a deeper comedy here: the timing of road repairs. They seem to happen at the most inconvenient moments, like on a Monday morning rush hour when Nairobians are already running late. There's something hilarious (and mildly tragic) about watching an entire workforce stuck in traffic because a road crew decided *that day* was the best time to dig up the tarmac. Priorities, right?

Yet, we persevere. With more projects underway, Kenya's road infrastructure is slowly evolving, bringing farmers closer to markets, tourists closer to attractions, and—most importantly—bringing Kenyans closer to each other. We just need to dodge a few potholes along the way.

When the Lights Go Out (Again): Kenya's Power Struggle

Nothing says "Kenya" quite like a power blackout at the most inconvenient moment. You're about to send an important email, the power goes out. You're in the middle of the latest episode of your favorite series, the power goes out. You blink, and guess what? *Power. Goes. Out.*

Kenya Power (the monopoly electricity provider) has unintentionally become a part of Kenyan humor. People have developed strategies for surviving outages that rival disaster preparedness plans. "Candles, power banks, and an infinite supply of jokes about Kenya Power" have become the trifecta of survival.

Now, don't get me wrong: Kenya has made remarkable strides in electrification. In fact, our national grid is quite impressive compared to many countries in the region. The growth of renewable energy, particularly through geothermal and wind power, has positioned Kenya as a leader in sustainable energy. Projects like the Olkaria Geothermal Power Plant and the Lake Turkana Wind Power Project are proof that Kenya is not just sitting around in the dark (most of the time).

But let's not sugarcoat it—while we're making great strides, power reliability is still a bit of a dice roll. It's the sort of situation where you invite friends over for a barbecue, and you spend half the time explaining that *"Yes, the power might go out, but don't worry, I've got enough firewood for the nyama choma."*

The good news? The future of Kenya's energy sector is looking brighter (pun intended). There are ongoing efforts to expand grid coverage to rural areas and ensure reliable power. Soon, we'll be able to laugh about the days when we depended on WhatsApp groups to alert us about blackouts, and maybe even move into a future where power cuts are as rare as a politician admitting fault.

Broadband Dreams: The Battle for Internet Connectivity

In the age of digital economies, having fast and reliable internet is as essential as oxygen. In Kenya, however, the battle for connectivity often feels like playing a game of hide and seek—sometimes the signal hides, and sometimes you seek (desperately). You know the drill: You're trying to load a video, and all you get is that infernal spinning wheel of doom. Or you're on a Zoom call, and your screen freezes at the precise moment your boss asks, *"Are you there?"*

That being said, Kenya has been hailed as one of Africa's leading countries in terms of internet access. Nairobi is home to an ever-growing number of tech companies, start-ups, and innovation hubs that rely on broadband. But while you can easily get Wi-Fi in most of Nairobi, go a little further into the rural areas, and things get sketchy. You might find yourself climbing a hill just to get a single bar of 3G (if you're lucky).

Still, broadband connectivity is transforming Kenya. From the booming e-commerce sector to the rise of online education and remote work, Kenyans are navigating a digital world with increasing confidence. The government's ambitious National Broadband Strategy aims to connect the entire country with high-speed internet by 2030, and while the skeptics may chuckle, the progress so far suggests that it's not entirely a pipe dream.

But let's not kid ourselves—when your Wi-Fi drops mid-Netflix marathon, it's hard not to scream, *"Why me, Lord?"* That frustration aside, the digital revolution in Kenya is unstoppable. Tech hubs like Konza Technopolis (dubbed the "Silicon Savannah") represent a bold vision for Kenya's future as a regional ICT hub. One day, we'll all look back and laugh about the days when "buffering" was part of the Kenyan vocabulary.

Building Bridges (And Not Just Politically)

In the realm of politics, "building bridges" has taken on a new meaning in Kenya. But let's talk about the literal bridges—the ones that keep us moving, quite literally, over rivers, valleys, and busy city streets.

Kenya has seen a steady increase in infrastructure projects aimed at improving transport and logistics. Take the Standard Gauge Railway (SGR) as an example. When the SGR launched, many Kenyans were skeptical. Who needed a modern railway when we had matatus and buses? But soon enough, the SGR became a beloved staple, allowing Kenyans to travel from Nairobi to Mombasa in comfort, all while enjoying the views of the savannah. Some might argue the best part of the SGR isn't the speed or convenience, but the fact that you can charge your phone the whole way without worrying about power outages.

Then there's the Nairobi Expressway, which, when it's not being turned into a mobile safari experience thanks to traffic, represents the changing face of Kenyan infrastructure. It's an ambitious project that has redefined urban transport, even if the tolls sometimes feel like you're paying for a one-way ticket to a tax bracket you don't belong in.

And bridges are about more than just steel and concrete. They connect people to opportunities. Farmers in rural Kenya now have better access to urban markets, and products can flow more efficiently across the country. The result? A more integrated economy, where the boundaries between "city life" and "village life" are becoming increasingly blurred. Sure, the potholes might still be there, but at least we're getting somewhere.

The Future of Kenya's Infrastructure: It's Gonna Be Big (And Hilarious)

As Kenya continues to develop its infrastructure, we can expect to see more ambitious projects, more pothole jokes, and, of course, more matatu drivers creatively navigating the chaos. From roads to broadband, power to bridges, we're building the foundation for a future where Kenya is not just surviving but thriving.

But as we look to the future, we must keep our sense of humor. After all, infrastructure in Kenya is a journey filled with twists, turns, bumps, and occasional detours. We may not have reached our final destination yet, but we're on the road—and trust me, the ride is worth every laugh.

Agriculture as a Pillar of Economic Development – Feeding the Nation, Feeding the World

In Kenya, agriculture is more than a way of life—it's a national obsession. You can't walk five minutes in the countryside without tripping over a farmer tending to their shamba (small farm) with the kind of dedication that would make a neurosurgeon look like a slacker. It's in our DNA. Ask any Kenyan about their plans for the future, and more often than not, you'll hear, "I'm thinking of starting a small farm, maybe plant some maize." It doesn't matter if they've never held a jembe (hoe) in their life—farming is the dream.

But let's be honest, agriculture in Kenya has its fair share of comedy gold. Whether it's rain falling exactly one hour after you give up on planting or watching a goat escape its pen with the agility of an Olympic sprinter, farming here is an adventure. However, beneath the humor lies a sector that is crucial to Kenya's survival and prosperity. Agriculture is Kenya's economic backbone, feeding millions and providing livelihoods for about 75% of the population. Yet, as much as we love farming, we must also face the fact that our traditional ways need an upgrade. Welcome to the hilarious and hopeful journey of modernizing Kenya's agriculture.

The Comedy of Traditional Farming

Let's start with the basics: traditional farming in Kenya. It's a world where the sight of a farmer manually plowing a field with two cows (who look like they'd rather be anywhere else) is still common. Forget about GPS-guided tractors—our farming methods are often closer to the Stone Age than the 21st century. But hey, it works, right? Well, sort of.

Take maize farming, for example, which is practically a national sport. The maize harvest is so important that it determines whether we eat ugali (a staple dish made from maize flour) in peace or spend the next six months rationing. Every year, farmers anxiously wait for the rains, which usually arrive fashionably late, like that friend who always shows up to a party when everyone else is leaving. When the rains do come, they either flood the fields or drizzle just enough to make the soil damp but useless. It's like nature is playing an elaborate prank on us.

Then there are the farm animals. Chickens that refuse to lay eggs, cows that somehow always end up in your neighbor's garden, and goats that behave more like escape artists than livestock. One minute you're counting your chickens (literally), and the next, they've all disappeared because you forgot to close the coop. Farming in Kenya is essentially a sitcom starring you, the animals, and Mother Nature, who never sticks to the script.

But as amusing as this might be, traditional farming methods can't feed a growing population or compete in the global market. It's time for a revolution—a technological, sustainable, and innovative one that turns Kenya's agricultural potential into an economic powerhouse.

Enter the Age of Smart Farming

Now, imagine this: a Kenyan farmer sitting on their shamba with a smartphone in one hand, a drone hovering above their maize field, and an app that tells them the exact time to water their crops. Welcome to the future of Kenyan farming—smart farming, where technology is transforming agriculture into a high-tech, data-driven industry.

Let's talk about drones. Once the domain of tech geeks and wedding photographers, drones are now flying over maize fields, taking pictures, analyzing soil quality, and monitoring crops for diseases. These little flying robots are the new generation of farmhands. While some farmers might still be figuring out how to unlock their smartphones without accidentally calling their entire contact list, others are already embracing these gadgets with open arms. "Mzee wa Drone," as he's affectionately called in one village, has become a local celebrity, known for zipping his drone over fields faster than a boda boda (motorbike taxi) during rush hour.

Next, we have precision agriculture—where farmers use data to make decisions instead of relying on gut feelings or "signs from the ancestors." With apps like DigiFarm and M-Farm, farmers can now access information on everything from weather patterns to market prices. They can even buy seeds and fertilizer online, because why bother going to the market when you can order everything from your phone while sipping tea? And if you're wondering whether Kenyan farmers are ready for this technological leap, just ask any farmer how they feel about M-Pesa (mobile money). If we can trust our entire banking system to a mobile app, we can certainly trust technology to help us grow better crops.

The beauty of smart farming is that it's not just for large-scale farmers. Small-scale farmers, who make up the majority of Kenya's agricultural sector, can also benefit. From solar-powered irrigation systems to mobile apps that offer farming tips in local languages, technology is leveling the playing field. It's like turning every farmer into a CEO of their own mini-agro empire, except with more chickens and fewer board meetings.

Sustainable Farming: The Only Way Forward

Now, while smart farming is exciting, we can't forget about sustainability. You see, Kenya's traditional farming methods have often leaned heavily on nature's resources—sometimes a bit too heavily. Deforestation, soil degradation, and overgrazing have led to environmental challenges that can't be ignored. Enter sustainable farming, the hero we didn't know we needed.

Sustainable farming isn't just about planting trees and hugging cows (though both are encouraged); it's about using resources in a way that ensures future generations will also have land to farm. The good news? Kenyan farmers are already embracing techniques like agroforestry, crop rotation, and organic farming. The bad news? Convincing your grandmother to switch from burning charcoal to using biogas is like trying to teach a chicken to swim—it's possible but requires some serious persuasion.

One of the most promising trends is the return to indigenous crops. Forget about importing everything from Europe—Kenya's climate is perfect for growing nutritious, drought-resistant crops like sorghum, millet, and cassava. These crops might not have the glitz and glamour of maize, but they're incredibly resilient and could help combat food insecurity in a country where the rains are as unreliable as Nairobi traffic.

Agribusiness: The Billion-Shilling Industry No One Saw Coming

Here's a fun fact: agriculture isn't just about feeding ourselves; it's also a potential goldmine. Agribusiness—farming with a business mindset—is taking off in Kenya, and it's not just about selling tomatoes at the local market anymore. We're talking about farmers exporting avocados to Europe, processing coffee for international brands, and producing honey that's more popular than the latest gospel hit.

Take the avocado craze, for example. Kenyan avocados are so good that they're being snapped up by European and Asian markets faster than you can say "guacamole." Some farmers have even switched from maize to avocados entirely, lured by the promise of export dollars and the chance to live the dream of being a global fruit mogul. And let's not forget flowers—Kenya's flower industry is blossoming (pun intended) with exports to places like the Netherlands. Imagine that: Kenyan roses in Dutch vases, all thanks to agribusiness.

But it's not just about exports. Agribusiness is also transforming how food is processed and sold locally. Farmers are setting up value-added businesses like yogurt factories, fruit juice processing plants, and even organic skincare lines made from farm-grown ingredients. In fact, the only thing that seems to be growing faster than Kenyan crops is Kenyan creativity. If you thought farming was just about planting seeds and waiting for rain, think again. Modern Kenyan farmers are entrepreneurs, strategists, and innovators rolled into one.

Feeding Kenya, Feeding the World

Here's the truth: Kenya is hungry. Not just in the literal sense (though hunger is still a major issue), but hungry for change. The country has vast agricultural potential, but it's clear that traditional methods alone won't cut it anymore. We need innovation, technology, sustainability, and a dash of humor to transform agriculture into a sector that doesn't just feed us, but feeds the world.

Kenya's role in global food security is no joke. With the right investments in infrastructure, education, and technology, we could become one of the leading food exporters in the world. Our fertile soils and diverse climate zones give us an edge, but we need to embrace modern practices and think big. And when we say big, we mean *feed-the-world* big.

Think about it: Kenyan farmers exporting organic coffee to Japan, supplying fresh vegetables to Middle Eastern markets, and filling European shelves with our world-class flowers and fruits. It's not just a dream—it's happening, slowly but surely. But we need to scale up, and that requires support from both the government and private investors who see the future of Kenya in its fields and farms.

The Future is Bright (And Delicious)
The future of Kenyan agriculture is like a perfectly ripe mango: bright, sweet, and full of potential. But like that mango, it can also be a bit tricky to navigate—there are challenges ahead, from climate change to market access. But if there's one thing Kenyan farmers know how to do, it's to persevere. With a little bit of humor, a lot of hard work, and the right tools, we can turn agriculture into the cornerstone of Kenya's economy.

In the end, whether we're growing avocados for export, using drones to monitor crops, or laughing about the latest goat escape, Kenyan agriculture is moving forward. And who knows? In a few years, we might just be the ones feeding not only Kenya but the world, one farm at a time.

So grab your jembe, update your farming app, and get ready. The future of farming in Kenya is here, and it's going to be as delicious as it is transformative.

Innovation in Public-Private Partnerships – A Collaborative Approach to Development

Kenya is a country that thrives on hustling. From roadside vendors selling roasted maize with one hand while making change with the other, to a boda boda (motorbike taxi) rider somehow navigating five lanes of traffic that don't even exist, Kenya is the land of improvisation. And nowhere is this spirit of innovation more evident than in the world of public-private partnerships (PPPs).

In theory, PPPs are about collaboration between the public sector (the government) and private enterprises to drive development and improve service delivery. But in Kenya, where every project comes with a little extra "flavor," PPPs are not just partnerships—they're like a matatu (public minibus) ride. You're not quite sure how it's going to go, there will be a lot of bumps along the way, but somehow, you'll end up getting where you need to be, possibly with some hilarious stories to tell.

Kenya's success in using PPPs to drive innovation, build infrastructure, and improve services is a testament to the country's ability to turn challenges into opportunities. It's a blend of bold ideas, strategic collaboration, and—of course—a touch of Kenyan humor. So let's dive into the sensational, often comedic world of public-private partnerships in Kenya and explore how these innovative collaborations are transforming the country.

Public Meets Private: Like Two Relatives at a Family Wedding

Picture a family wedding where two distant relatives, the slightly disorganized but well-meaning government auntie and the slick, well-dressed private enterprise uncle, are forced to work together to make the event a success. Auntie is in charge of logistics but keeps misplacing the guest list, while Uncle is great with finances but insists on giving a speech at every opportunity. Now imagine that the wedding is Kenya's economy, and these two relatives have to collaborate to get the country's development plans off the ground.

Welcome to the world of public-private partnerships, where the public sector and private businesses work together to deliver projects that neither could handle alone. Whether it's building roads, improving healthcare, or expanding internet connectivity, the idea behind PPPs is simple: combine the public sector's mandate to serve the people with the private sector's efficiency, innovation, and (hopefully) money.
But in true Kenyan style, nothing is ever as straightforward as it seems. Getting the public and private sectors to work together can sometimes feel like a stand-off between two matatu drivers, each convinced that they have the right of way. The government often has grand ideas but lacks the financial muscle or expertise to execute them, while the private sector can be wary of the government's notorious red tape and bureaucracy.

Still, when the two sides come together, magical things happen. Take the Standard Gauge Railway (SGR), for example—a massive infrastructure project that would have been impossible without the collaboration between the Kenyan government and private enterprises. Sure, there were delays, controversies, and a few eyebrow-raising budget figures, but in the end, the train is up and running. And, let's be honest, how many Kenyans can say they've taken a selfie on the SGR and posted it with the hashtag #Progress?

The Road to Innovation: Where PPPs Pave the Way (Literally)

When it comes to infrastructure, PPPs have become Kenya's go-to solution for solving the country's growing need for better roads, bridges, and public utilities. The logic is simple: the government doesn't always have the money to build a shiny new highway or bridge, so they invite private companies to chip in with funding, expertise, and construction. In return, the private sector gets to make some profit through tolls, fees, or long-term contracts. It's like hiring a professional wedding planner because you know if you try to do it yourself, the cake might end up being served at midnight.

Take the Nairobi Expressway, for example, a partnership between the Kenyan government and private investors that promised to reduce Nairobi's legendary traffic jams. For those unfamiliar with Nairobi traffic, it's not just a daily commute—it's a test of patience, willpower, and your ability to invent new curse words. The Expressway was designed to alleviate some of this madness, allowing motorists to bypass traffic bottlenecks. In exchange, drivers have to pay a toll, but let's be real—when you've spent half your life stuck in traffic, the idea of paying to speed things up feels like a reasonable bargain.

Of course, like any good Kenyan project, the Nairobi Expressway has its share of comedic moments. The toll system itself sparked plenty of jokes. Some Nairobians found themselves enthusiastically tapping their M-Pesa accounts to pay the toll, only to later realize they had overestimated how much time it would actually save them. *"I paid all that to move from Lang'ata to Westlands in 10 minutes, and then spent an hour getting off the exit? Sawa tu!"* But overall, the project has been hailed as a success, proving that when the public and private sectors work together, the results can be transformational.

But roads aren't the only area where PPPs have had a major impact. Kenya's energy sector has also benefited tremendously from public-private collaboration. Projects like the Lake Turkana Wind Power Project—a joint effort between the Kenyan government and private investors—are helping to make Kenya a leader in renewable energy. Thanks to this project, Kenya is now home to the largest wind farm in Africa, contributing to the country's green energy goals and reducing our reliance on fossil fuels. Who knew that the same winds that used to blow dust into our faces could now power our homes?

Service Delivery: When PPPs Bring Health, Internet, and Water

PPPs aren't just about building roads and power plants—they're also about improving service delivery in sectors like healthcare, education, and even internet access. The idea is that by leveraging private sector innovation and efficiency, essential services can be delivered more effectively and reach more Kenyans. It's like the public sector is the chef with all the ingredients, and the private sector is the sous-chef who knows how to cook up a gourmet meal without burning down the kitchen.

Take healthcare, for example. Kenya's healthcare system has historically been underfunded and overburdened, with public hospitals often stretched to their limits. Enter PPPs, where private companies step in to provide funding, technology, and expertise, while the government ensures that the services reach those who need them most. In some cases, private companies are partnering with county governments to build hospitals or provide medical equipment, making healthcare more accessible to rural communities.

One standout example is the partnership between Philips (yes, the electronics company) and the Kenyan government to establish "healthcare hubs" in remote areas. These hubs provide basic healthcare services and are equipped with solar-powered diagnostic tools—because, let's face it, in some parts of Kenya, the power supply is about as reliable as a politician's promises.
Another area where PPPs are making a big difference is internet connectivity. Kenya is known as Africa's "Silicon Savannah," but not everyone has access to fast, reliable internet—especially in rural areas. Through PPPs, companies like Safaricom and Liquid Telecom are partnering with the government to expand broadband infrastructure, bringing internet access to parts of the country that previously had to rely on pigeons to deliver messages (just kidding, but it's close).

Thanks to these partnerships, schools, businesses, and households across the country are getting connected to the digital world. And with that connection comes opportunity—whether it's students accessing online learning materials, farmers using mobile apps to monitor market prices, or small businesses reaching customers through e-commerce platforms. It's as if the whole country has leveled up, and now even the most remote village can order goods online and have them delivered… sometime next week, if the boda boda guy doesn't get lost.

The PPPs of the Future: Bold Ideas and Even Bolder Strategies

Kenya's public-private partnerships have come a long way, but the future promises even more exciting (and sometimes hilarious) possibilities. As the country looks to address challenges like affordable housing, sustainable agriculture, and climate change, PPPs will continue to play a crucial role. And if there's one thing we know about Kenyans, it's that we can make even the most serious projects entertaining.

Take affordable housing, for example. The Kenyan government has ambitious plans to build 500,000 affordable homes, but financing and logistics are a challenge. Enter PPPs, where private developers collaborate with the government to build housing projects that are not only affordable but also modern, eco-friendly, and stylish (because even in a PPP, Kenyans want to look good). The idea is that the private sector brings in investment and construction expertise, while the government ensures the homes are accessible to middle- and low-income earners. Of course, if you ask Kenyans about it, they'll likely say something like, *"Niko na nyumba, lakini ile kitu inauma ni mortgage"* (I have a house, but what hurts is the mortgage).

Sustainable agriculture is another area where PPPs are making waves. With a growing population and the looming threat of climate change, Kenya's agricultural sector needs innovation more than ever. Through partnerships with private companies, the government is introducing technology like drought-resistant seeds, smart irrigation systems, and digital tools that help farmers predict weather patterns and market trends. Who knew farming could become so high-tech? Soon enough, we'll be seeing grandmas in rural Kenya checking their phones for soil moisture updates while plowing their fields.

And speaking of technology, Kenya's tech sector is ripe for more public-private collaboration. As more Kenyan startups emerge in the fields of fintech, healthtech, and agritech, the potential for PPPs to drive innovation is huge. Imagine a future where a Kenyan startup partners with the government to create a nationwide app for paying taxes, renewing licenses, and reporting potholes—actually, scratch that, we'd need an app solely dedicated to potholes. *"Pothole 254: Spot a pothole, get it fixed, thank us later."*

The Challenges (and Comedy) of PPPs

Of course, no discussion about PPPs would be complete without acknowledging the challenges—and, in true Kenyan fashion, the comedy that often comes with them. From endless bureaucracy to budget overruns, PPPs can sometimes feel like trying to herd cats while juggling pineapples.

One of the biggest challenges is the dreaded "red tape." Ask anyone who's ever tried to do business with the government, and they'll tell you about the endless forms, approvals, and meetings that seem to stretch on forever. PPPs are no different. Sometimes, a project will get stuck in the approval phase for so long that by the time it's ready to launch, the technology has already moved on, and everyone's wondering why we're still using floppy disks.

Then there's the issue of accountability. As with any collaboration, there's always the potential for things to go wrong. Maybe the private partner cuts corners to save costs, or the government partner "loses" a few million shillings somewhere along the way. In Kenya, these mishaps often end up in the headlines, sparking jokes, memes, and plenty of public outrage. *"Nani aliiba pesa za Expressway? Tunataka kujua kama kuna toll fees za pesa pia"* (Who stole the Expressway money? We want to know if there are toll fees for cash as well).

But despite the challenges—and the comedy—public-private partnerships are one of Kenya's best tools for driving innovation and development. When done right, they can deliver infrastructure, services, and opportunities that benefit all Kenyans, from the bustling streets of Nairobi to the quiet villages of Mandera.

Conclusion: The Future is Bright (and Hilarious)

As Kenya continues to grow and develop, public-private partnerships will remain a key part of the country's strategy for success. Whether it's building roads, expanding healthcare, or connecting more people to the internet, PPPs are helping to create a better future for all Kenyans.

And while the journey might come with a few bumps, a lot of laughs, and the occasional "did they really just do that?" moment, one thing is clear: when the public and private sectors work together, anything is possible—even a matatu ride with seat belts.

So here's to more innovation, more collaboration, and more hilarious stories about how Kenya's public-private partnerships are making our country a better place, one project at a time.

Building Financial Discipline – From Consumption to Savings and Investment

Ladies and gentlemen, it's time to talk about everyone's favorite subject—**money**! Yes, that magical thing we all dream of but somehow never seem to have enough of. It comes into our lives with a lot of promises, but before we know it, it disappears faster than the last piece of nyama choma at a family gathering. One minute you're thinking, "This is the month I'll finally start saving," and the next thing you know, you're staring at a mountain of M-Pesa withdrawal fees and wondering how you managed to spend Ksh 1,500 on "delivery fees" for a takeout burger.

Welcome to **Kenya's spending culture**, where we all want to live like millionaires without actually saving a single shilling. But don't worry, dear reader, you're not alone. We've all been there—blowing through our salaries in record time, hoping for that **last-minute miracle** from somewhere (read: a generous friend or relative). But here's the thing: living like that isn't sustainable. In fact, it's downright dangerous. So, grab your calculators (or at least pretend you have one), because today we're going to explore how to shift from a **spending culture to one of saving and investment**—and trust me, we'll have some fun along the way.

Shifting from a Spending Culture to One of Saving and Investment

Let's start with the cold, hard truth: **we love to spend**. From Nairobi's high-end malls to the local kiosks, Kenyans are always ready to "treat themselves." Whether it's the latest phone upgrade, the trendiest shoes, or that overpriced coffee that somehow makes us feel more important, we're addicted to consumption. And don't even get me started on the number of times we've gone out for drinks with friends, only to wake up the next day with nothing but an empty wallet and a headache.

But here's the million-shilling question: why do we spend so much? Well, it's because we've been conditioned to believe that **owning things equals success**. And hey, who doesn't want to look successful? But here's the kicker: **real success isn't about how much you spend—it's about how much you save and invest**. Because let's be honest, your designer shoes won't pay your rent when you're retired, and your brand-new iPhone won't grow your wealth. So, it's time to flip the script and shift from spending to **saving and investing**.

Imagine this: instead of blowing through your salary on impulse purchases, what if you put aside 20% of your income every month into a **savings account**? And what if, instead of splurging on that third pair of sneakers, you invested in the **stock market** or a **small business**? Suddenly, your money wouldn't just be working for you— it would be growing. The power of **compound interest** is like having a little financial genie working behind the scenes, multiplying your savings while you sleep. And no, you don't need to be an economics expert to get started. You just need a plan—and some willpower.

Financial Literacy as a Driver of Personal and National Prosperity

Now, let's talk about the big, scary monster that too many people are afraid of: **financial literacy**. I know, the term sounds boring and maybe even a little intimidating, like something that only accountants and bankers care about. But the truth is, **financial literacy is the key to building**

personal wealth—and it's also the key to making Kenya a financially prosperous nation.

Let's face it, most of us didn't grow up learning about savings, investments, or how to manage debt. We learned how to **spend**—and we learned how to spend well. But we didn't learn how to make our money work for us. Financial literacy is like that magic decoder ring you need to figure out the mysteries of money. Without it, you're flying blind, hoping that your good looks and charm will somehow lead to financial stability (spoiler alert: they won't).

So, what exactly is financial literacy? It's the ability to **understand and manage your money wisely**. It's knowing how to budget, how to save, how to invest, and how to avoid debt traps like a pro. It's being able to look at your bank statement without breaking into a cold sweat. And the best part? **Anyone can learn it**. You don't need to be a math genius or have a degree in finance. All you need is the willingness to take control of your money instead of letting it control you.

Imagine if every Kenyan had a basic understanding of personal finance. We'd be living in a country where people weren't drowning in debt, where savings rates were high, and where everyone had a plan for their future. And guess what? That kind of personal financial discipline would lead to a **stronger national economy**. When citizens save and invest, they create capital for businesses to grow, jobs to be created, and the economy to flourish. It's a win-win situation—and it all starts with financial literacy.

Community Savings Groups and Cooperatives as Tools for Empowerment

Now that we've established the importance of financial literacy, let's talk about one of the most effective (and, dare I say, fun) ways to build wealth: **community savings groups and cooperatives**. If you think saving money on your own is tough, try doing it with a group of people who have your back and are just as committed to financial empowerment as you are.

You see, in Kenya, we've got a secret weapon that most people don't realize: **chamas** (informal savings groups) and **SACCOs** (Savings and Credit Cooperative Organizations). These groups are financial game-changers, and they've been helping people save, invest, and grow their wealth for decades. Think of them as the original **crowdfunding platforms**, long before anyone ever heard of GoFundMe.

Chamas: The Unsung Heroes of Savings

Let's start with **chamas**, the small savings groups that are as Kenyan as chapati and tea. A chama is basically a group of people—often friends, family, or neighbors—who come together to pool their resources and save money collectively. Every month, each member contributes a set amount of money, and the group decides how to use the funds, whether it's for personal savings, investments, or a group business venture.

Now, here's where it gets interesting: chamas aren't just about saving—they're about **empowerment**. These groups give people access to funds they might not be able to get from traditional banks. Want to start a small business but don't have the capital? Your chama's got your back. Need a loan to pay for school fees? Boom—chama to the rescue. And the best part? You're not just a borrower—you're also

an investor, meaning that as your chama grows, so does
your wealth.

SACCOs: The Big Leagues of Cooperative Banking

If chamas are the grassroots of financial empowerment,
then **SACCOs** are the big leagues. SACCOs are
cooperative financial institutions where members pool their
savings and can take out loans at reasonable interest rates.
Unlike banks, SACCOs are owned by their members,
which means that all the profits go back to the people—not
to some faceless corporation.

SACCOs have been instrumental in helping Kenyans,
especially in rural areas, gain access to affordable credit.
Whether it's for farming equipment, home improvements,
or starting a business, SACCOs are there to provide the
financial boost that people need. And the best part?
SACCOs encourage financial discipline. Members are
required to save regularly, and they can only borrow based
on how much they've saved, which keeps people from
getting into unmanageable debt.

So, whether you're part of a chama or a SACCO, the point
is this: **community savings groups work**. They empower
people to take control of their financial futures, build
wealth, and invest in themselves and their communities.
And the best part? You're not doing it alone—you've got a
whole team cheering you on.

Practical Tips for Long-Term Wealth Building

Now that we've covered the importance of saving and the power of community savings groups, let's get down to the nitty-gritty: **practical tips for building long-term wealth**. Because at the end of the day, it's not about how much money you make—it's about how much you keep, invest, and grow.

1. Budget Like a Boss

First things first: if you don't have a **budget**, you're basically driving blindfolded. A budget is your financial GPS—it tells you where your money is going and helps you stay on track. Start by listing all your monthly income (yes, including that side hustle selling second-hand clothes) and then list all your expenses. Break it down into categories: essentials (like rent, food, and utilities), savings, and discretionary spending (you know, those Friday night drinks). The goal is to make sure you're living within your means and **saving at least 20%** of your income each month.

2. Pay Yourself First

This is one of the oldest tricks in the book, but it works like magic: **pay yourself first**. Before you start paying bills or buying groceries, take a portion of your income and put it straight into savings or investments. Treat it like a non-negotiable expense. This way, you're prioritizing your future before you start spending on your present.

3. Start Investing Early

You don't need to be a financial guru to start investing—you just need to get started. Whether it's buying shares in the stock market, investing in government bonds, or even starting a small side business, the key is to **put your money**

to work. The earlier you start investing, the more time your money has to grow. Remember, wealth-building is a marathon, not a sprint.

4. Avoid Unnecessary Debt

Debt is like that friend who's fun at first but then overstays their welcome and eats all your food. If you don't manage it properly, it can ruin your financial future. Avoid taking out loans for things you don't need (looking at you, impulse car buyers), and always make sure you can comfortably repay any debt you take on. If you're already in debt, focus on paying it off as quickly as possible, starting with the high-interest ones.

5. Create Multiple Streams of Income

One of the best ways to build long-term wealth is to **diversify your income streams**. Don't rely on just one source of income (because, let's be honest, jobs aren't as secure as they used to be). Whether it's starting a side hustle, investing in real estate, or selling handmade crafts on Instagram, having multiple streams of income will help you grow your wealth faster and provide a safety net in case one stream dries up.

Conclusion: From Consumption to Wealth Creation

So, what's the big takeaway? **Building financial discipline isn't just about saving money—it's about changing your mindset.** It's about shifting from a culture of consumption to a culture of **investment and growth**. It's about educating yourself on personal finance, getting involved in community savings groups, and making smart choices that will set you up for long-term success.

Kenya's future prosperity depends on each and every one of us learning how to manage our money wisely, invest for the future, and build wealth that lasts. So, the next time you're tempted to buy that shiny new gadget you don't need, remember this: **true wealth isn't about what you buy—it's about what you build**.

Now go out there and start building your financial empire. The future is rich—literally!

KEYPOINTS AND SUMMARY

Job Market Struggles: Kenyan graduates face a tight job market, with prolonged job-seeking frustrations.

Entrepreneurship as a Solution: Instead of job-seeking, entrepreneurship offers opportunities for innovation, job creation, and economic growth.

National Development Benefits: Entrepreneurs drive job creation, innovation, economic growth, and poverty reduction.

Cultural Shift Needed: Promote risk-taking, creativity, collaboration, and entrepreneurship education to foster innovation.

Successful Kenyan Entrepreneurs: Stories of Mike Macharia (Seven Seas Technologies), Tabitha Karanja (Keroche Breweries), and Peter Njonjo (Twiga Foods) illustrate entrepreneurship's transformative power.

Future of Entrepreneurship: Entrepreneurship is key to Kenya's development and individual empowerment.

Kenya's Digital Revolution: While facing challenges like outdated systems, Kenya is on the verge of a tech transformation, from e-government to AI.

Digital Literacy Growth: WhatsApp dominates communication, but more Kenyans are embracing coding, tech hubs, and online education.

Tech and Innovation Hubs: iHub and Gearbox lead Kenya's innovation, producing solutions like mobile apps that enhance daily life.

E-Government and Governance: Digitalizing government services aims to eliminate bureaucratic inefficiencies.

Tech in Education: Digital learning is empowering students with coding and global knowledge.

Silicon Savannah: Kenya is emerging as Africa's tech hub, with homegrown innovations transforming the economy.

Kenya's Infrastructure Challenges: Roads with potholes, unreliable power, and inconsistent internet highlight the country's infrastructure problems.

Road Network: Kenya's roads, though often poorly maintained, are essential for connecting rural areas and boosting trade, with major projects like the LAPSSET corridor offering hope.

Power Struggles: Despite progress in renewable energy, power blackouts are common, affecting daily life.

Internet Connectivity: Kenya is a leader in Africa's digital space, but rural broadband lags behind urban areas.

Future Vision: Major projects like the SGR and Nairobi Expressway symbolize Kenya's potential for infrastructure growth and economic development.

Agriculture's Importance: Agriculture is Kenya's economic backbone, with 75% of the population relying on it for livelihoods.

Challenges in Traditional Farming: Outdated methods and unpredictable weather make farming inefficient, highlighting the need for modernization.

Smart Farming: Technology like drones, mobile apps, and precision agriculture is revolutionizing the sector, making farming more efficient.

Sustainability: Sustainable practices, such as agroforestry and indigenous crops, are crucial for long-term food security.

Agribusiness Growth: Agribusiness is booming, with Kenya exporting avocados, flowers, and processed goods.

Global Potential: With innovation, Kenya could become a major global food exporter.

Kenya's Hustle and Innovation: PPPs embody Kenya's spirit of improvisation, driving development through collaboration between the government and private sector.

Infrastructure Success: Projects like the Standard Gauge Railway and Nairobi Expressway showcase how PPPs improve roads and reduce traffic.

Energy and Services: PPPs contribute to renewable energy projects like the Lake Turkana Wind Farm and expand healthcare and internet access.

Future PPPs: Focus on affordable housing, sustainable agriculture, and tech innovation.

Challenges and Humor: Bureaucracy, accountability issues, and Kenyan humor add complexity, but PPPs remain key for development.

Kenya's Spending Culture: Many prioritize consumption over saving, with a focus on material success rather than financial security.

Shift to Saving and Investment: Encourages shifting from spending to saving and investing for long-term wealth.

Financial Literacy: Essential for managing money, avoiding debt, and contributing to national prosperity.

Community Savings Groups: Chamas and SACCOs empower individuals to save, invest, and grow wealth collectively.

Practical Wealth-Building Tips: Budgeting, investing early, avoiding unnecessary debt, and creating multiple income streams are key strategies.

Mindset Shift: True financial success comes from a focus on long-term growth, not short-term consumption.

Healing Our Land – Sustainability and Environmental Stewardship

Ladies and gentlemen, boys and girls, gather 'round because we're about to embark on a wild, hilarious, and slightly disturbing ride through the land of climate change and environmental stewardship. Yes, we're talking about saving the planet—or, more specifically, **Kenya**—from the environmental apocalypse that's been sneaking up on us faster than the traffic on Thika Road at rush hour.

Let's be real: you've heard the words "climate change" thrown around more times than you've heard the phrase "hakuna matata," but have you ever stopped to think about what it means for **Kenya's development**? It's not just about polar bears losing their homes (although that's tragic too); it's about our farms drying up, rivers turning into mud puddles, and somehow experiencing droughts and floods at the same time. Climate change is like that unwelcome relative who never leaves and somehow makes everything worse, yet we're all pretending we can live with it.

But before you roll your eyes and scroll to the next chapter, stick with me. This isn't just another preachy piece about how you need to plant trees and save the turtles (although, spoiler alert: you really should). This is about **sustainability**—the thing that could transform our country, heal our land, and, dare I say, make Kenya the envy of the world (okay, at least East Africa).

So grab your reusable water bottle, put on your solar-powered hat (it's a thing, look it up), and let's dive into why **sustainability** is not only important but actually kind of cool—and maybe even hilarious if you squint at it the right way.

The Impact of Climate Change on Kenya's Development

Now, let's start with a little reality check: **climate change is real, people.** No matter how many times you hear someone say, "But it was cold last week!" (That's not how it works, Karen). The truth is, Kenya is feeling the heat, literally and figuratively. We're not just talking about the scorching sun that makes you regret ever leaving your house; we're talking about the effects of climate change on **agriculture, water resources, infrastructure, and, let's face it, our overall vibe**.

First, let's talk about **agriculture**, which is, you know, kind of a big deal around here. Agriculture accounts for roughly 30% of Kenya's GDP and employs about 75% of the population. That means when the weather decides to throw a tantrum, it's not just the farmers who suffer—it's the entire country. Droughts have become as regular as matatu fare hikes, and floods seem to arrive like uninvited guests, leaving destruction in their wake. Crops fail, livestock dies, and we all start to feel the pinch when food prices soar.

But wait, there's more! **Water resources**—or should I say the lack of them—are becoming a major problem. Our rivers are shrinking, our lakes are drying up, and let's not even get started on Nairobi's water shortages. (Side note: If you've ever experienced Nairobi without water for a week, you know it's the stuff of nightmares). Climate change is turning what was already a water-scarce country into something resembling a desert, and that's bad news for development. After all, you can't build industries or sustain communities without water.

Now, let's talk about **infrastructure**, because nothing says "progress" like a bridge collapsing under the weight of floodwaters. Climate change doesn't just affect farms and forests—it also wreaks havoc on our roads, bridges, and buildings. Ever driven through a flooded street that looks more like a river? Yeah, that's climate change laughing in your face while you contemplate selling your car for a canoe.

And here's the kicker: **Kenya is trying to develop, but climate change is like that one cousin who keeps ruining family gatherings by spilling drinks on everyone's clothes.** We're making progress, but every time we take two steps forward, a drought, flood, or heatwave knocks us three steps back.

Shifting to Sustainable Agricultural Practices

Okay, enough with the doom and gloom. Let's talk solutions. If we want to save our land (and, let's be real, our livelihoods), we need to **shift to sustainable agricultural practices** faster than a Kenyan politician promises free Wi-Fi during election season.

Now, I know what you're thinking: "Sustainable agriculture? Isn't that just a fancy way of telling farmers to stop using pesticides and go organic?" Well, yes and no. It's more than that. Sustainable agriculture is about **finding ways to farm that don't deplete the land, waste water, or require us to use chemicals that sound like they belong in a sci-fi horror movie.**

Let's break it down:
1. **Water Conservation**: It's time to stop treating water like an unlimited resource and start acting like the precious gem it is. Farmers can use drip

irrigation, rainwater harvesting, and other methods to conserve water and keep crops hydrated without draining rivers and lakes dry. Imagine a world where we don't have to choose between taking a shower and watering crops. Wild, right?

2. **Agroforestry**: Yes, I'm about to suggest we plant more trees, but hear me out. Trees aren't just there to look pretty—they help improve soil quality, retain water, and even provide shade for crops. Plus, agroforestry is like the Swiss Army knife of farming: it's good for the environment, boosts crop yields, and gives farmers additional income through timber or fruit sales. Everyone wins, except maybe deforestation.

3. **Crop Rotation and Diversification**: Remember that scene in your high school science class where the teacher talked about crop rotation and you thought, "I'll never need to know this"? Well, it turns out it's kind of a big deal. By rotating crops and diversifying what we grow, we can prevent soil depletion, reduce the need for chemical fertilizers, and keep our farms more resilient to climate change. And, bonus: we get to eat a wider variety of foods instead of just maize, maize, and more maize.

4. **Organic Farming**: I know, I know—organic farming sounds like something hipsters in Lavington are obsessed with, but there's a reason it's becoming more popular. Organic farming reduces the use of harmful pesticides and fertilizers, keeps the soil healthier, and is better for the environment overall. Plus, have you ever eaten an organic tomato? It tastes like a real tomato, not

whatever those pale, flavorless things from the supermarket are pretending to be.

Community-Driven Environmental Protection Initiatives

Now, let's take a moment to give a **standing ovation to communities across Kenya** who are stepping up and saying, "Enough is enough!" when it comes to environmental destruction. These are the real heroes of our story—the everyday citizens who are doing their part to protect the environment without waiting for the government to roll out some complicated, bureaucratic initiative.

One of the coolest examples is **Wangari Maathai**, who, by the way, was not only a legend but also a Nobel Prize-winning environmentalist. She started the **Green Belt Movement**, which encouraged communities to plant trees, protect forests, and promote sustainable land use. Thanks to her movement, millions of trees have been planted, and local communities have benefited from the improved environment.

But it doesn't stop there. Across the country, **community-driven environmental initiatives** are popping up like mushrooms after a rainstorm. These initiatives range from community cleanup drives (because, let's be honest, Nairobi could use fewer plastic bags flying around) to groups focused on cleaning up rivers and forests. There's even a movement to clean up **Lake Victoria**, which is plagued by pollution and invasive species like the dreaded water hyacinth that's basically turned the lake into a green nightmare.

Here's the thing: **When communities come together to protect the environment, magic happens.** It's like a superhero team-up, but instead of fighting villains, they're fighting pollution, deforestation, and climate change. And the best part? These initiatives often have ripple effects—cleaner rivers mean better fish stocks, healthier forests mean more rainfall, and less pollution means fewer people getting sick from contaminated water. Everyone benefits, except maybe the water hyacinth (but I doubt it's reading this, so we're good).

The Role of Every Citizen in Preserving the Environment
So, where do you come in, dear reader? You might be thinking, "This all sounds great, but I'm not a farmer or an environmental activist. What can I do?" Well, let me tell you: **you have a role to play, and it's more important than you think**.

Let's start with the basics. Do you know that feeling when you finish a packet of crisps and absentmindedly toss the wrapper out of the car window? Yeah, that's a problem. Littering is like the gateway drug to environmental destruction, and we've all been guilty of it at some point. But no more! **Pick up your trash**. Recycle when you can. If you see a piece of trash on the street, pick it up (and maybe give the litterbug who dropped it a disapproving glare).

Next, let's talk about **water conservation**. Remember that time you let the tap run while you were brushing your teeth? That's right, I'm onto you. Water is life, and we need to treat it like the precious resource it is. Fix that leaky faucet, use water sparingly, and—if you're feeling ambitious—install a rainwater harvesting system at home.

Not only will you save water, but you'll also impress your neighbors with your eco-friendly setup.

And don't even get me started on **single-use plastics**. The amount of plastic waste we generate is enough to make an elephant cry. Say no to plastic bags, straws, and those plastic bottles that seem to multiply like rabbits. Instead, invest in reusable bags, metal straws, and a good water bottle. Not only will you help the environment, but you'll also look super cool carrying around your eco-friendly gear (okay, maybe not, but it's worth a shot).

Finally, one of the most important things you can do is **raise awareness**. Talk to your friends and family about environmental issues. Share articles, start discussions, and get involved in community initiatives. When more people are informed and engaged, change happens. It's like planting a seed of knowledge and watching it grow into a forest of action.

Saving Kenya, One Tree at a Time

At the end of the day, **healing our land** isn't just a nice idea—it's an absolute necessity. Climate change is knocking on our door, and unless we get our act together, it's going to kick that door down and leave us with nothing but dust and regret. But the good news is that we can do something about it. Whether it's shifting to sustainable agriculture, getting involved in community-driven initiatives, or simply picking up our trash, every little bit helps.

The fate of Kenya's environment isn't just in the hands of politicians or environmental activists—it's in your hands, my friend. So, let's get out there, plant some trees, conserve some water, and, most importantly, **stop treating our**

planet like it's disposable. Kenya is a beautiful, vibrant country, and it's up to all of us to keep it that way.

And who knows? Maybe one day, when we're all living in a lush, green Kenya with clean rivers and thriving forests, we'll look back and say, "We did that." Now, wouldn't that be something?

Tourism and Conservation – Harnessing Kenya's Natural Beauty for Economic Growth

If Kenya were a person, she'd be that friend who always has a picturesque view no matter where you visit. One day, she's chilling in the savannah, casually hanging out with elephants and lions. The next, she's up in the highlands, showing off lush tea plantations that stretch to the horizon. Later, you'll find her lounging on pristine beaches along the coast, with the Indian Ocean lapping at her feet like she's on an eternal vacation. In short, Kenya is the Beyoncé of the natural world—always looking stunning, always making you wonder how she does it.

But while Kenya is blessed with jaw-dropping natural beauty, she doesn't just sit there looking pretty. No, no, no—Kenya has learned to monetize her beauty, turning those rolling hills, vast savannahs, and tropical beaches into cash cows that bring in millions of dollars every year. And here's the kicker: this isn't just about taking a good selfie with a giraffe. It's about sustainable tourism, wildlife conservation, and eco-tourism—buzzwords that not only make you sound fancy at cocktail parties but also hold the key to preserving Kenya's natural heritage for future generations.

So, grab your safari hat, put on your virtual sunscreen, and let's take a wild, hilarious, and eye-opening tour through Kenya's tourism and conservation efforts. Spoiler alert: there will be lions, a few jokes about tourists, and a lot of good-natured poking fun at the quirks of trying to balance conservation and economic growth in a country that sometimes feels like the wildlife is in charge (and we humans are just visiting).

The Tourist Invasion: When Lions Have Paparazzi

Picture this: a lion lounging under an acacia tree, lazily flicking its tail as it surveys the savannah. It's a scene straight out of *The Lion King*, majestic and serene. Now, add a convoy of safari jeeps, each packed with tourists, all frantically snapping photos, their cameras clicking away like the lion is a Hollywood celebrity on the red carpet. The lion glances over at the spectacle, yawns, and goes back to sleep, utterly unimpressed. Welcome to Kenya's tourism scene, where the wildlife is used to being treated like royalty and the tourists are the paparazzi.

Kenya's wildlife is the star of the show when it comes to tourism, and rightfully so. Our national parks and game reserves, like Maasai Mara, Amboseli, and Tsavo, are home to some of the most iconic animals on the planet: elephants, lions, rhinos, giraffes, and cheetahs, to name a few. People fly in from all over the world just to catch a glimpse of a lion on the hunt or an elephant taking a casual mud bath. It's like the animal version of keeping up with the Kardashians, except way cooler.

But while tourists get to enjoy the thrill of seeing these animals in their natural habitats, the animals themselves have developed a certain… indifference to the whole thing. Take the wildebeest migration, for example. Every year, thousands of tourists flock to the Maasai Mara to witness the Great Migration, where millions of wildebeest and zebras cross the Mara River in one of nature's most awe-inspiring spectacles. The tourists are there with their binoculars, cameras, and safari gear, gasping in wonder. The wildebeest, on the other hand, are just trying to get to the other side without becoming lunch for a crocodile. It's another day at the office for them.

But here's the twist: while the animals might be indifferent, tourism is a big deal for Kenya's economy. In fact, tourism accounts for a significant chunk of the country's GDP, bringing in billions of shillings each year. From high-end luxury lodges in the heart of the savannah to budget backpacker camps on the coast, tourism creates jobs, generates revenue, and helps boost local economies. But here's where things get tricky: how do we balance the influx of tourists with the need to protect our wildlife and preserve the very beauty that attracts them in the first place?

When Conservation Becomes a Comedy of Errors

Conservation in Kenya is serious business. We're talking about saving endangered species, protecting ecosystems, and ensuring that future generations will still be able to enjoy the breathtaking beauty of our national parks. But like most things in Kenya, even conservation comes with its fair share of hilarity.

Take, for instance, the phenomenon of "problem animals." This is the term used when wild animals decide to leave their designated national park and take a little stroll into human territory. Picture this: you're a farmer tending to your crops when, out of nowhere, an elephant shows up like it's been invited to lunch. You panic, knowing full well that a single elephant can flatten your entire shamba (farm) in a matter of minutes. You run to call the Kenya Wildlife Service (KWS), who show up with a truck, a tranquilizer dart, and a lot of optimism. The result is usually a comical standoff between humans and animals, with the elephant being tranquilized and carefully transported back to the park, looking rather grumpy about the whole ordeal.

Then there's the case of the infamous Nairobi traffic jam caused by lions. Yes, you read that right. One fine day, a few lions from Nairobi National Park decided to go for a walk—right onto one of the city's major highways. Chaos ensued, as cars screeched to a halt and people began filming the lions from the safety of their vehicles. Nairobians were stuck in a traffic jam (nothing new there), but this time the reason was far more exciting than usual. KWS eventually showed up to escort the lions back to the park, but not before the story went viral, with headlines like "Lions Cause Traffic Jam" making the rounds on social media. It was the most Nairobi thing ever.

Despite the comedy, conservation is a matter of life and death for many species. Kenya is home to several critically endangered animals, including the black rhino and the Grevy's zebra. Poaching remains a major threat, particularly for rhinos and elephants, whose horns and tusks are highly sought after on the black market. The fight against poaching is intense, with KWS rangers risking their lives to protect these animals. Kenya has taken strong steps, including passing strict anti-poaching laws and working with international organizations to combat illegal wildlife trade.

But here's where the humor sneaks in again: in some instances, conservation efforts can feel like a constant game of cat and mouse (or, more accurately, ranger and poacher). Rangers patrol vast areas of land, sometimes spending days tracking down poachers who use increasingly sophisticated techniques to evade capture. In one case, a group of poachers tried to smuggle ivory out of the country disguised as a shipment of avocados. Let that sink in for a moment. Ivory. As avocados. You have to admire their creativity, even if it was a terrible plan.

Eco-Tourism: When Tourists Become Conservationists (Whether They Like It or Not)

Eco-tourism is the new buzzword in Kenya's tourism industry, and it's more than just a fancy way to market eco-lodges. The idea behind eco-tourism is simple: create tourism experiences that not only allow visitors to enjoy Kenya's natural beauty but also contribute to conservation efforts. In other words, come for the lions, stay for the tree-planting ceremony.

One of the best examples of eco-tourism in action is in the Maasai Mara, where local Maasai communities have partnered with conservation organizations to create eco-friendly lodges that directly benefit both the environment and the local people. Tourists can stay in luxurious tented camps, go on guided safaris with Maasai warriors, and even participate in community projects like building schools or digging wells. It's a win-win situation: the tourists get an unforgettable experience, the local community earns a livelihood, and the wildlife is protected.

Of course, not all tourists are prepared for the reality of eco-tourism. Take the case of a group of city-dwelling tourists who signed up for an "authentic bush experience," expecting a weekend of Instagram-worthy sunsets and cute baby elephants. What they didn't expect was the power outage that left them without Wi-Fi for 48 hours or the cheeky vervet monkeys that raided their breakfast table. They returned to the city with stories of how they "survived

the wild," but in truth, the monkeys were more of a threat
to their pancakes than any predator lurking in the bush.

But beyond the laughs, eco-tourism is playing a critical role
in sustainable development. By involving local
communities in conservation efforts and ensuring that
tourism revenue is reinvested in environmental protection,
Kenya is setting an example for the world on how to
harness natural beauty for economic growth while
safeguarding it for future generations.

The Future of Conservation: More Tech, Less Drama

Kenya's approach to conservation is constantly evolving,
and the future looks bright—if a little high-tech. From
drones monitoring wildlife in remote areas to GPS collars
that track the movements of endangered animals,
technology is revolutionizing how we protect our natural
heritage. Conservationists are using everything from
satellite imagery to artificial intelligence to keep tabs on
wildlife populations and combat poaching.

In some cases, technology is being used in unexpected
ways. Take, for instance, the use of elephant collars that
can send text messages to rangers when an elephant strays
too close to a human settlement. Yes, you heard that
right—text messages. Imagine getting a text from an
elephant. "Hey, I'm heading towards your farm. You might
want to move your crops."

But while technology is a powerful tool, it's not a silver
bullet. The real key to successful conservation lies in
education and awareness. More and more Kenyans are
recognizing the importance of protecting our natural

resources, not just for tourism but for the well-being of the country as a whole. Schools are incorporating environmental education into their curricula, and campaigns like "Ivory Belongs to Elephants" are raising awareness about the impact of poaching.

The Circle of Life: Keeping the Balance

At the heart of tourism and conservation in Kenya is the need to strike a balance—between economic growth and environmental protection, between human development and wildlife preservation. It's a delicate dance, but one that Kenya is well-positioned to lead. Our natural beauty is a treasure, and with the right policies, strategies, and a bit of humor, we can ensure that it continues to shine for generations to come.

So, whether you're a tourist snapping selfies with giraffes or a conservationist tracking rhinos with a drone, remember this: Kenya's beauty isn't just a backdrop for adventure. It's a living, breathing ecosystem that needs our protection—and maybe a little bit of our laughter along the way.

After all, who can resist laughing at the sight of a lion holding up traffic in Nairobi? Only in Kenya, my friends. Only in Kenya.

Housing for All – Tackling Urbanization and Affordable Housing

Kenya is urbanizing faster than you can say, "Nairobi rent hike." Every day, people pour into cities in search of better opportunities, better jobs, and perhaps, if they're really lucky, a house where the plumbing works, the ceiling doesn't leak, and you don't share your apartment with three uninvited rats and an equally unwelcome cockroach family. But as the cities grow, so do the challenges—chief among them being the question that haunts every Kenyan: **"Where am I going to live?"**

It's the classic urban housing problem, and it's happening everywhere from the bustling streets of Nairobi to the rapidly expanding towns of Eldoret, Mombasa, and Kisumu. With Kenya's population set to hit 66 million by 2030, it's like trying to cram the entire country into a one-bedroom flat—something's got to give. Tackling urbanization and providing affordable housing is the biggest balancing act the country is facing today. It's a bit like trying to perform a magic trick where you pull affordable, decent housing out of a hat—except you forgot the hat, the audience is a million-strong, and someone just tripled the price of construction materials.

So how do we solve this housing crisis? How do we make sure that everyone has a roof over their head that doesn't collapse at the first sign of rain? Join me as we explore the wild, hilarious, and ultimately inspiring world of urbanization and affordable housing in Kenya, where sustainable urban planning meets the Kenyan spirit of improvisation (and where you might still have to deal with a few surprise rats).

The Nairobi Rent Olympics: May the Odds Be Ever in Your Favor

Ah, Nairobi—the city where opportunity meets chaos, where the skyline is filled with cranes, and where rent prices defy all logic. Finding affordable housing in Nairobi is like participating in the Rent Olympics, where only the strongest, smartest, and most cunning renters survive. You start with high hopes, scrolling through online listings that describe every tiny flat as "spacious" and every broken-down building as "vintage." By the end, you're negotiating with a landlord who somehow thinks it's reasonable to charge you KSh 50,000 for a studio the size of a cupboard.

The housing situation in Nairobi has become so extreme that the search for a place to live has turned into a national pastime. Whether it's endless apartment viewings where you discover that "ample parking" means you'll be fighting for space with 20 other cars, or the realization that "running water" is more of a suggestion than a guarantee, Nairobians have learned to laugh through the pain.

But behind the jokes and memes lies a very real problem. Urbanization is outpacing the ability of cities to provide adequate housing, and as more people flood into urban centers, the demand for affordable accommodation is skyrocketing. In Nairobi alone, the population is expected to reach 6 million by 2030, and most of these new residents will be low- to middle-income earners. The current housing stock simply can't keep up, and for many, the only option is to settle in informal settlements, where access to basic services is a daily struggle.

The Kibera Dilemma: Informal Settlements and the Search for Dignity

No discussion of housing in Kenya is complete without mentioning Kibera, Nairobi's largest informal settlement and, depending on who you ask, either a testament to human resilience or an indictment of failed urban planning. Kibera is home to an estimated 250,000 people, crammed into an area of just 2.5 square kilometers. The houses are made from corrugated iron sheets, with narrow alleys that wind through a maze of structures that look like they might topple over with a strong gust of wind. It's a place where the toilet situation is—let's say—**"complicated."**

Yet despite the challenges, Kibera is a vibrant, bustling community. Life goes on, and people find ways to make it work. But let's be honest: no one should have to live like this. The rise of informal settlements like Kibera highlights the glaring gap in affordable housing, and the government has a responsibility to step up and provide solutions that offer dignity and decency to all citizens.

Kenya's affordable housing plan aims to address this by building 500,000 new affordable homes across the country by 2022 (spoiler alert: we didn't hit that target, but the effort continues). The goal is to provide decent housing for the millions of Kenyans who are priced out of the formal housing market. But there's a big difference between announcing a plan and making it a reality. As anyone who's ever tried to build a house in Kenya knows, the road from blueprint to finished product is long and filled with more delays than a Nairobi traffic jam.

Affordable Housing: The Kenyan Dream (with a Side of Mortgage Stress)

In a country where owning a home is seen as the ultimate dream, the prospect of affordable housing is enough to make most Kenyans perk up faster than they would at the sight of a free plate of nyama choma. But the truth is, the word "affordable" is relative. What's affordable to one person might seem outrageously expensive to another, and the concept of "affordable housing" in Kenya often comes with a catch.

Take, for example, the ambitious affordable housing projects currently being developed in Nairobi and other cities. These new estates promise modern, well-planned communities with decent amenities, all within reach of the average Kenyan. The catch? You'll need to sign up for a mortgage, and unless you've got a secret stash of cash under your mattress, that mortgage will take a hefty chunk out of your salary for the next 20-30 years.

The very idea of a mortgage sends chills down the spine of most Kenyans. Many of us grew up watching our parents build houses one brick at a time, literally paying as they went—whether it took 5 years or 15 years. So the thought of signing up for a long-term mortgage with monthly payments that rival your food budget is, to put it mildly, a bit terrifying. But if the alternative is spending your life renting a flat where the landlord refuses to fix the broken bathroom door, the mortgage suddenly starts to look a lot more appealing.

The Green Building Craze: Sustainable Urban Planning (with a Kenyan Twist)

As Kenya's cities expand, there's a growing recognition that we can't just throw up buildings willy-nilly and hope for the best. Sustainable urban planning is the new buzzword, and while it sounds fancy, it's basically about building cities that don't collapse under the weight of their own growth. The idea is to create livable, walkable, and environmentally friendly communities where people can work, play, and live without constantly worrying about traffic jams, pollution, or flooding.

Kenya is beginning to embrace the idea of "green buildings"—structures designed to minimize environmental impact through energy efficiency, sustainable materials, and eco-friendly design. From solar panels on rooftops to rainwater harvesting systems, the goal is to create housing that's both affordable and kind to the planet. The best part? Green buildings are no longer just the preserve of high-end estates with names like "Whispering Palms" or "Sunset Villas." Affordable housing projects are starting to incorporate these features, meaning that even low-income families can live in homes that are environmentally sustainable.

One of the best examples of sustainable urban planning in action is Konza Technopolis, Kenya's planned "smart city" located just outside Nairobi. Dubbed "Silicon Savannah," Konza is designed to be a futuristic city that integrates technology, green spaces, and sustainable design to create a community where people can live and work without battling Nairobi's chaotic traffic. Of course, the project has faced delays (this is Kenya, after all), but the vision is there, and it's a sign that Kenya is starting to think about the future of urban development in a smart way.

But let's not kid ourselves—sustainable urban planning in Kenya also comes with its share of challenges. The classic Kenyan approach to urban planning is to build first and ask questions later, often resulting in roads that abruptly end in someone's living room or drainage systems that flood at the first sign of rain. Creating livable cities that can handle the rapid pace of urbanization will require more than just green buildings and fancy buzzwords—it will take long-term planning, investment in infrastructure, and, of course, a little bit of Kenyan improvisation.

The Boda Boda Question: Transporting People and Livelihoods

No conversation about urbanization and housing would be complete without mentioning one of Kenya's most iconic features: the boda boda. These motorbike taxis are the lifeblood of the country's cities and towns, ferrying people, goods, and even the occasional goat through traffic-clogged streets with remarkable speed (and, let's be honest, a healthy dose of fearlessness). But as cities grow, the question becomes: how do we integrate transport solutions like boda bodas into sustainable urban planning?
Boda bodas are both a blessing and a curse. On one hand, they provide an essential service, helping people navigate the maze of urban streets with speed and efficiency. On the other hand, they're also a bit of a menace, weaving in and out of traffic, often ignoring traffic rules, and contributing to the chaos of urban life. As cities expand and the demand for housing grows, finding a way to incorporate transport solutions like boda bodas into the urban fabric will be key to creating livable cities.

Some urban planners are already experimenting with "boda-friendly" housing developments that include designated parking areas and dedicated boda lanes. It's a small step, but it's a recognition that boda bodas aren't going anywhere anytime soon, and they'll need to be part of the solution if we're going to create cities that work for everyone.

Housing for All: The Kenyan Dream (Yes, Even for You)

At the end of the day, the dream of affordable housing isn't just about brick and mortar—it's about creating communities where people can thrive. It's about giving Kenyans the opportunity to own a home without having to sell their kidney to pay the mortgage. It's about making sure that cities are livable, sustainable, and inclusive for everyone—from the middle-class office worker in Nairobi to the small-scale trader in Kisumu.

Kenya's urbanization challenges are huge, but so are the opportunities. With the right mix of innovation, strategic planning, and good old-fashioned Kenyan hustle, we can create cities that not only meet the housing needs of the growing population but also provide a high quality of life for all residents.

So whether you're looking for a flat in Nairobi, a house in Eldoret, or a plot of land in Machakos, take heart: housing for all is not just a pipe dream. It's a goal that Kenya is working towards with humor, resilience, and a few unexpected surprises along the way. And who knows? Maybe one day, you'll finally find that perfect home where the water runs, the ceiling doesn't leak, and the only rats around are the ones on your neighbor's plot.

Rural Development – Bridging the Gap Between Urban and Rural Kenya

If Kenya were a movie, the storyline would revolve around the contrast between its bustling cities and peaceful rural areas. On one side, we've got Nairobi, where the pace of life is like that of a matatu weaving through traffic—fast, chaotic, and occasionally nerve-wracking. On the other side, there's rural Kenya, where life flows at a more relaxed pace, punctuated by the sound of cows mooing, farmers working the fields, and roosters waking up everyone before the sun has even thought about rising. It's a tale of two worlds, and like any good drama, it's all about bridging the gap.

For decades, the development of Kenya has been something of an urban-centric affair. Cities like Nairobi, Mombasa, and Kisumu have flourished, their skylines dotted with new skyscrapers and the streets filled with ambitious young Kenyans looking to make their mark. Meanwhile, rural Kenya has often been left feeling like the forgotten sibling, holding down the fort while everyone else goes off to chase the bright lights. But here's the twist—rural Kenya is not just sitting idly by. It's demanding its share of the spotlight, and there's a growing realization that without rural development, national progress is incomplete.

In this chapter, we'll explore the sensational, often hilarious, and sometimes absurd story of rural development in Kenya. From policies that aim to reduce disparities between urban and rural areas, to the humorous realities of trying to bring high-tech solutions to a village with more goats than people, this is a journey of transformation, empowerment, and the occasional head-scratching moment. So put on your gumboots (because we're going to the farm), pack your sense of humor, and let's dive into the wonderful world of rural development in Kenya.

The Urban-Rural Divide: Nairobi vs. the Village (A Tale of Two Worlds)

If you've ever traveled from Nairobi to rural Kenya, you know the experience is a bit like entering a parallel universe. In the city, life moves at breakneck speed. There's a new restaurant opening every week, the traffic is impossible, and everyone's talking about *"hustling"* as if it's a national sport. Then, two hours into your journey to the village, you're greeted by something entirely different—lush green fields, children playing by the roadside, and that one cow that seems to think the road is its personal grazing spot.

The contrast between urban and rural Kenya is stark, and the disparities are equally jarring. In cities, access to amenities like electricity, clean water, healthcare, and schools is relatively easy. You can order pizza online, get an Uber in five minutes, and Wi-Fi is practically a human right. Meanwhile, in many rural areas, basic services can still be a struggle. Potholes the size of swimming pools, electricity that comes and goes as it pleases, and healthcare centers that are more "suggestions" than actual functioning facilities are part of everyday life.

But while urban areas have raced ahead with development, rural Kenya is no slouch. Rural areas are the backbone of the country's agriculture, feeding millions and generating the majority of Kenya's exports. The real challenge is making sure that this powerhouse of potential gets the infrastructure and opportunities it deserves.

Bridging the Gap: When Development Heads to the Shamba

For years, the government has recognized the need to bridge the gap between urban and rural Kenya. The question is: how do you bring modern infrastructure, education, and healthcare to an area where the nearest town is 50 kilometers away, and the local mode of transport is either a boda boda or, if you're feeling fancy, a donkey cart?

The solution lies in rural development policies that aim to create equitable growth for all Kenyans, whether they live in the bustling heart of Nairobi or the tranquil hills of Nandi County. One of the key initiatives is **devolution**, which was introduced by Kenya's 2010 constitution. Devolution handed significant powers to county governments, allowing local leaders to direct development projects in their areas based on the specific needs of their communities. In theory, it's a brilliant plan. In practice? Well, it's a bit like giving everyone the same recipe for cooking ugali and then watching how differently each county interprets it.

Some counties have used devolution to great effect. In areas like Makueni County, where the governor prioritized healthcare, residents now enjoy access to fully functioning hospitals, maternity wards, and healthcare services that rival those in urban areas. Other counties, well… let's just say their priorities are still a work in progress. You might find a county that's built an impressive governor's mansion while the local school is still waiting on proper toilets.

But devolution is just one part of the equation. National projects like **rural electrification** have also played a huge role in bridging the gap between urban and rural areas. The government's efforts to extend the electricity grid to rural communities have been met with both excitement and humor. One story goes that when a village in western Kenya finally got electricity, the first thing one elder did was plug in his radio and turn up the volume to the max—because what's the point of electricity if your whole village can't hear the latest news?

And then there's the issue of **water access**. In many rural areas, fetching water is still a daily chore that involves walking long distances with jerry cans balanced on your head. Enter various government and NGO initiatives to provide boreholes, wells, and rainwater harvesting systems. But in true Kenyan fashion, things don't always go smoothly. One particularly infamous incident involved a water tank meant for a community project being delivered but somehow ending up as the chief's new "personal rainwater collector"—because, of course, what's development without a little bit of drama?

The Tech Revolution Goes Rural: When Wi-Fi Meets the Village Goat

Rural Kenya isn't just about farms and cows anymore—it's becoming a hotspot for innovation and technology. In recent years, tech companies, start-ups, and the government have launched initiatives to bring digital solutions to rural areas, from mobile banking platforms to e-learning tools. But as you can imagine, introducing high-tech solutions to areas where the local population is more concerned with the price of fertilizer than the latest iPhone comes with its fair share of hilarious moments.

Take, for example, the rollout of mobile banking in rural areas. While services like **M-Pesa** have transformed how

Kenyans send and receive money, there was a time when trying to explain mobile money to an elder in the village was a comedy show in itself. One story goes that a well-meaning son set up his elderly father with an M-Pesa account, only for the father to keep asking where the actual money was. "How can I trust this thing if I can't see the coins?" he allegedly asked, suspiciously poking at his phone like it was about to explode.

But jokes aside, technology has been a game-changer for rural development. Farmers can now access market prices in real-time, students in remote areas can learn online, and mobile health clinics are using telemedicine to provide consultations in areas without doctors. And while the image of a farmer on a boda boda checking his crop prices via smartphone may seem funny, it's also a symbol of progress—because this is the future of rural Kenya.

Agriculture: The Backbone of Rural Development

Let's not forget the core of rural Kenya: agriculture. Kenya's rural areas are the breadbasket of the nation, producing everything from tea and coffee to maize and potatoes. But for too long, farmers have been left to their own devices, often facing poor infrastructure, lack of access to credit, and fluctuating market prices that make farming a risky business.

Enter **agribusiness**—the new frontier in rural development. By treating farming as a business rather than a subsistence activity, rural communities are transforming their agricultural practices to increase productivity and profitability. Tech start-ups are developing apps that connect farmers directly with buyers, cutting out the middlemen who often take the lion's share of the profits. And programs like **One Acre Fund** are providing farmers with seeds, tools, and training to maximize yields.

One particularly amusing (and slightly sad) example of how rural farming is changing comes from a farmer in the Rift Valley who, after attending an agribusiness seminar, realized that his cows had been producing half the milk they should have been. His solution? He named his cows "High Productivity" and "Low Productivity" to keep track of their milk output—because sometimes, you just need to give your cows a motivational name.

The Importance of Education: Schools in the Village, and the Case of the Missing Chalk

If you've ever been to a rural Kenyan school, you know that while the spirit of learning is alive and well, the infrastructure can leave a lot to be desired. Schools often operate with limited resources, teachers are underpaid, and in some cases, students still sit on logs for lack of desks. The urban-rural education divide is real, and it's one of the biggest barriers to equitable development.

In response, the government has launched several initiatives aimed at improving education in rural areas. The **Free Primary Education** program, launched in 2003, was a huge step forward, but challenges remain, especially when it comes to quality. While urban schools have computers and science labs, rural schools are sometimes lucky to have enough chalk for the blackboard.

Yet despite these challenges, rural students are proving that they can compete with the best of them. From students in

Turkana County scoring top marks in national exams to young inventors in rural schools creating innovative solutions to local problems, the potential is there. What's needed is more investment in school infrastructure, teacher training, and digital learning tools to level the playing field.

Of course, in true Kenyan style, education comes with its own set of amusing stories. Take the time when a school in western Kenya received laptops as part of the **Digital Literacy Programme**, only for the teachers to lock them in the storeroom because they didn't know how to use them. "We were waiting for someone to come and explain how they work," one teacher admitted. Technology is great, but only if you know what to do with it!

The Road Ahead: Toward Equitable Development

The future of rural Kenya is bright, but getting there will require a concerted effort from both the government and the private sector. Policies that promote rural infrastructure development, improve access to education and healthcare, and support agriculture as a business are essential to closing the gap between urban and rural areas.

But beyond the policies and initiatives, rural development is also about changing mindsets. It's about recognizing that rural Kenya isn't just a place for retirees or farmers—it's the heartbeat of the country. It's where the food is grown, where traditions are preserved, and where innovation is just waiting to take root.

As Kenya continues to develop, we must ensure that no one is left behind. Whether you're a farmer in the foothills of Mount Kenya or a tech entrepreneur in the heart of Nairobi, you're part of the same story—the story of Kenya's progress.

So here's to rural Kenya—where life moves at its own pace, where challenges are met with resilience, and where the future is as bright as the morning sun over the fields. With the right investment, the right policies, and a healthy dose of Kenyan humor, we can bridge the gap between urban and rural Kenya once and for all. And who knows? Maybe one day, the village will be the new city, and we'll all be rushing there to get away from the traffic.

KEYPOINTS AND SUMMARY

Impact of Climate Change on Kenya: Climate change is affecting agriculture, water resources, and infrastructure, leading to droughts, floods, and rising food prices.

Sustainable Agricultural Practices: Solutions include water conservation, agroforestry, crop rotation, and organic farming to improve resilience.

Community-Driven Initiatives: Local communities play a vital role in environmental protection, exemplified by the Green Belt Movement and clean-up efforts.

Citizen Responsibility: Every individual can contribute by reducing litter, conserving water, and avoiding single-use plastics.

Call to Action: Kenya's environmental future relies on collective action, from planting trees to advocating for sustainability.

Kenya's Natural Beauty: Kenya's stunning landscapes, from savannahs to beaches, draw tourists and fuel the economy.

Tourism's Economic Impact: Tourism is a significant contributor to Kenya's GDP, attracting global visitors for wildlife and natural experiences.

Conservation Challenges: Balancing tourism with wildlife conservation is essential, with humorous situations like elephants in farms and lions causing traffic jams.

Eco-Tourism: Encourages sustainable tourism that benefits local communities and protects the environment.

Technological Solutions: Innovations like drones and GPS collars help monitor wildlife and combat poaching.

Future Focus: Emphasis on education and technology to maintain the balance between economic growth and conservation.

Rapid Urbanization: Kenya is urbanizing quickly, creating a growing demand for affordable housing, especially in cities like Nairobi, Eldoret, and Mombasa.

Housing Crisis: Finding affordable housing is a major challenge, with many forced into informal settlements like Kibera, highlighting the gap in housing supply.

Affordable Housing Efforts: Government initiatives aim to build 500,000 affordable homes, but challenges such as high costs and mortgage stress persist.

Sustainable Urban Planning: Emphasizes green buildings and sustainable communities like Konza Technopolis, integrating eco-friendly solutions.

Transport Solutions: Boda bodas play a key role in urban transport, requiring better integration into city planning for livability.

Urban-Rural Divide: Highlights the stark contrast between fast-paced urban cities like Nairobi and the relaxed rural areas.

Rural Development Importance: Rural Kenya is vital for agriculture and national progress but has been neglected in infrastructure and services.

Devolution's Impact: Devolution has empowered counties to prioritize local development, but results vary greatly across regions.

Tech in Rural Areas: Technology is transforming rural Kenya with mobile banking, e-learning, and agriculture apps.

Agriculture as a Business: Farmers are shifting to agribusiness, improving productivity and profits.

Education: Rural schools face resource challenges, but students show great potential.

Future Vision: Equitable development requires investment in infrastructure, education, and agriculture to bridge the urban-rural gap.

A Unified Kenya – Overcoming Tribalism and Fostering National Cohesion

Ladies and gentlemen, boys and girls, welcome to the greatest show in the world: **The Great Kenyan Tribal Circus!** Okay, maybe that's a bit of an exaggeration, but honestly, sometimes it feels like we're all living in a reality TV show where the contestants are divided into tribes, and the prize for the winner is… well, absolutely nothing. Except for maybe bragging rights and the right to say "I told you so" at family gatherings.

But here's the thing: **tribalism is not a game**, and it's certainly not something we can afford to keep playing. If you think of Kenya as one big family, then tribalism is that one relative who always shows up at family events and ruins everything. You know the one—they start drama, stir up old grudges, and somehow always manage to leave the room messier than they found it. Well, it's time for that relative to leave and never come back, because we have bigger fish to fry, like **building a united Kenya** where everyone is rowing in the same direction and not constantly poking holes in the boat.

So, let's dive into **the historical roots of tribalism**, why diversity can actually be our greatest strength, and how we can overcome this seemingly insurmountable challenge to foster **national cohesion**. And, of course, we'll do it with a healthy dose of humor, because if we can't laugh at our problems, we'll just end up crying into our ugali.

Understanding the Historical Roots of Tribalism in Kenya

To understand why tribalism is such a big deal in Kenya, we have to take a little trip down **memory lane**. Don't worry, we won't stay long—it's a bumpy road with a lot of potholes, but it's important to know where this whole mess started.

Once upon a time, before Kenya was even a country, people lived in various communities based on their ethnic groups. You had the Kikuyu, the Luo, the Kalenjin, the Luhya, and a whole bunch of others doing their own thing. They were farming, fishing, herding cattle, and occasionally engaging in friendly neighborhood disputes over who had the best roast goat recipe.

But then along came the British with their imperialist hats and a strange fascination with tea plantations. They decided to slap all these ethnic groups together and call it a country. And just like that, **Kenya was born**—a patchwork of tribes forced to live under one roof like an uncomfortable family reunion where no one knows who's bringing the dessert.

The colonial government, being the delightful people they were, decided to **divide and rule**. They stoked the fires of tribalism by favoring certain ethnic groups over others, creating divisions that would last long after they packed their bags and left. And when Kenya finally gained independence, we were left to pick up the pieces of a fractured society. The colonial powers may have left, but the tribalism they encouraged stuck around like a bad odor.

Fast forward to today, and tribalism is still alive and kicking. It shows up in our politics, our workplaces, and even in our social interactions. It's like that annoying mosquito that keeps buzzing around your ear no matter how many times you try to swat it away. But here's the kicker: **we don't need tribalism**. In fact, it's holding us back. So let's figure out how to squash this mosquito once and for all.

How Diversity Can Be a Strength Rather Than a Dividing Line

Here's a fun fact: **Kenya has 42 different ethnic groups**. That's right—42! Think about that for a second. Most countries would kill for that level of diversity. It's like walking into a buffet where there's every kind of food imaginable, and instead of enjoying the variety, we're all fighting over the ugali. Madness, right?

Now, I get it. Tribal identities run deep. They're a part of who we are, and there's nothing wrong with celebrating your culture and heritage. But here's where we've gone wrong: instead of using our diversity as a strength, we've let it divide us. We've fallen into the trap of thinking that just because someone speaks a different language or comes from a different region, they're somehow "the other."

But let me tell you something: **diversity is our superpower**. When you bring together people from different backgrounds, with different ideas, experiences, and perspectives, amazing things can happen. Diversity isn't a weakness—it's an advantage. It's what makes us resilient, creative, and innovative. It's the secret sauce that can take Kenya from being just another country on the map to being a global leader in business, technology, and culture.

Take a look at any successful company, and you'll see that they thrive on diversity. Different people bring different strengths to the table. It's like forming a superhero team— if everyone had the same power, you'd be in trouble. Imagine if the Avengers were all just a bunch of guys with shields. Boring, right? But throw in a billionaire tech genius, a guy who turns into a giant green monster, and a

Norse god, and suddenly you've got a team that can take on anything.

The same goes for Kenya. We don't need to be divided by our differences—we need to embrace them. When we come together as a united nation, we're stronger than ever. We can solve problems more creatively, build businesses that cater to a wide range of people, and create a society where everyone feels like they belong. And honestly, wouldn't that be a lot more fun than constantly bickering over who's from which tribe?

Fostering Inter-Ethnic Collaboration in Politics, Business, and Community

Now that we've established that **diversity is awesome**, let's talk about how we can foster **inter-ethnic collaboration** in all the areas that matter—**politics, business, and community.**

Let's start with the obvious one: **politics**. Ah yes, Kenyan politics—where tribalism has more airtime than a soap opera. Every election cycle, we're treated to the same old script: politicians rallying their tribal bases, making promises they can't keep, and stirring up ethnic divisions like they're making a pot of githeri. It's exhausting.

But here's the thing: **we don't have to play their game**. Politicians only use tribalism because it works for them. If we stop voting along tribal lines and start voting based on competence, integrity, and policies that actually benefit everyone, tribalism will lose its power. It's that simple. Imagine a Kenya where politicians have to actually earn votes by doing their jobs instead of relying on tribal loyalties. Wild, right? But it's possible.

Now let's talk about **business**. If there's one area where tribalism has no place, it's the business world. Why? Because money doesn't care where you're from. When you're running a business, the only thing that matters is whether you can deliver a quality product or service. In fact, some of the most successful businesses in Kenya are the ones that bring together people from different ethnic backgrounds to work toward a common goal.

Take, for example, the tech industry. Nairobi's **Silicon Savannah** is booming, and it's not because people are sticking to their tribes. It's because entrepreneurs, engineers, and developers from all over the country are collaborating to create cutting-edge technology that's putting Kenya on the map. They're not asking, "Where are you from?" They're asking, "What skills do you bring to the table?" And that's how it should be.

Finally, let's talk about **community**. Tribalism can feel especially entrenched at the local level, where people tend to stick to their own ethnic groups out of habit or comfort. But communities are where real change happens, and if we want to overcome tribalism, we need to start at home.

One way to foster inter-ethnic collaboration in communities is through **shared projects**. Whether it's building a school, cleaning up a neighborhood, or starting a community garden, when people from different ethnic groups work together, they build relationships, trust, and a sense of shared purpose. It's hard to hold onto stereotypes about "those people" when you're digging holes together and sharing a plate of chapati at the end of the day.

The Role of Media, Schools, and Leaders in Promoting Unity

Now, let's talk about the **heavy hitters**—the institutions that have the power to shape how we see ourselves and each other: **media, schools, and leaders**.

Let's start with **media**. Kenyan media has a massive role to play in either perpetuating or dismantling tribalism. Too often, we see headlines that pit one tribe against another, or hear talk show hosts subtly (or not so subtly) stoking ethnic tensions. But it doesn't have to be that way. Imagine if media outlets made a conscious effort to highlight stories of unity, collaboration, and cross-cultural friendship. Imagine if instead of focusing on our differences, they celebrated what brings us together. It would be like watching the news and actually feeling good about the future for once!

Now onto **schools**. If we want to create a more unified Kenya, we have to start with the next generation. Schools are the perfect place to teach kids that tribalism is a relic of the past, and that they're part of something much bigger—**a united Kenyan identity**. This can be done through curriculum changes, intercultural exchanges, and programs that encourage students from different ethnic backgrounds to work together on projects.

And last but not least, **leaders**. Politicians, religious leaders, community leaders—they all have a responsibility to promote unity instead of division. Leaders set the tone for the rest of society, and if they're constantly using tribalism to their advantage, it sends the message that division is acceptable. But when leaders rise above tribalism and actively work to bring people together, they create a ripple effect that can transform the entire country.

Conclusion: The Kenya We Deserve

So, what's the bottom line? **Kenya doesn't need tribalism**. We don't need the divisions, the stereotypes, or the petty rivalries. What we need is **unity**. We need to embrace our diversity and use it as a strength, not a weakness. We need to collaborate across ethnic lines in politics, business, and community. And we need to demand that our media, schools, and leaders promote unity instead of division.

It's not going to happen overnight, but if we all make a conscious effort to overcome tribalism, we can build the Kenya we deserve—a Kenya where everyone, no matter their tribe, has a seat at the table.

And wouldn't that be something? A country where unity, not division, is the name of the game. A Kenya where we can finally stop arguing about who makes the best roast goat and just enjoy the meal together. **Hakuna matata**, indeed!

Sports and Culture – Uniting a Nation Through Shared Heritage

There's something magical about sports and culture in Kenya. It's the way they cut across all divides—tribal, political, economic—and somehow, make us all feel part of something bigger than ourselves. Whether it's the sheer thrill of watching **Eliud Kipchoge** fly down a marathon course like a gazelle in Nike shoes, or the communal pride felt when Kenyan traditional songs are performed on global stages, there's no denying that **sports and culture unite Kenyans** like little else can.

Kenya may be known around the world for its breathtaking safaris and world-class long-distance runners, but the story of our **sports and cultural identity** runs much deeper. From dusty football pitches in the rural areas to the pulsating beats of local music in Nairobi clubs, sports and culture play a pivotal role in shaping our national identity, keeping our spirits high, and—most importantly—**giving us something to argue about when politics gets too heated**.

In this chapter, we'll dive into the wonderful world of Kenyan sports and culture, exploring how they've become symbols of unity, pride, and good old-fashioned fun. We'll look at why sports and culture matter so much to us, why every Kenyan fancies themselves a football expert during the World Cup, and why, deep down, even the most stoic of us will tear up when we hear a Maasai warrior chant. And of course, we'll do it all with a healthy dose of humor because, well, this is Kenya, and if we can't laugh at ourselves, then who can?

The Marathon of Life: Why Running is in Our Blood (Literally)

If there's one thing Kenya is known for around the world, it's running. Long-distance running, to be precise. In fact, if you're Kenyan and someone finds out, the first thing they'll ask is, "Oh, so are you a marathoner?" To which you will politely smile and say, "Well, not exactly, but I can run for a matatu when necessary."

Kenyans dominate the world of long-distance running like no other country. Whether it's the **Olympics**, the **Boston Marathon**, or Eliud Kipchoge's unbelievable **sub-two-hour marathon** feat, Kenya consistently produces champions who make the entire nation swell with pride. And while many of us can barely run a kilometer without collapsing into a wheezing heap, we feel a sense of ownership over the achievements of our athletes. When Kipchoge wins, it's as though we all won—sitting on our couches, drinking tea, but spiritually crossing that finish line alongside him.

The phenomenon of Kenyan runners is often ascribed to a combination of **altitude, genetics, and sheer willpower**. But let's be honest, part of the reason is that **running is life** for many Kenyans. In the highlands of **Iten** and **Eldoret**, children run to school (uphill both ways, as they'll remind you) and sprint home afterward to help with chores. There's no Uber to pick them up and drop them off at practice; it's all about using your own two legs—and if those legs happen to be capable of winning a marathon someday, all the better.

But beyond the accolades and medals, **running is a symbol of Kenyan resilience**. It represents our ability to push through challenges, to keep going even when the path is tough, and to never give up. Whether we're cheering for our athletes from the stands or from our living rooms, there's a deep sense of unity and pride that comes from knowing that, as a nation, we're capable of greatness.

Football: Kenya's National Sport (of Watching, Not Winning)

Ah, football (or **soccer**, for those who insist on being difficult). There's no denying that football is the **real heartbeat** of sports culture in Kenya. And while our national team, **Harambee Stars**, has given us more headaches than heartwarming moments, it's the sport that unites Kenyans like nothing else. Just try going to a bar in Nairobi during an **English Premier League (EPL)** match, and you'll see exactly what I mean.

Kenyans take football seriously. Very seriously. Ask any random Kenyan about football, and suddenly you'll find yourself in a 30-minute conversation where they'll explain the intricate details of **Liverpool's** tactical errors in the 1984 European Cup, as if they were right there on the bench. EPL loyalties run deep here, and you'll often see Kenyans sporting jerseys of their favorite teams— **Manchester United**, **Arsenal**, and **Chelsea** being the most popular. In fact, during football season, Nairobi might as well be a satellite office of the EPL, with every conversation inevitably drifting towards the latest scores and player transfers.

But why, you may ask, do we put so much emotional investment into foreign football leagues when our own national team is… well, let's just say "struggling" is a generous term? The truth is, **Harambee Stars** have mastered the art of dashing our hopes at the most critical moments. Yet, we remain loyal. We show up. We cheer. We complain (loudly). And when, by some miracle, they manage to win a match, it feels like Christmas has come early. And let's not forget our women's football team, the **Harambee Starlets**, who have given us moments of genuine joy and pride, showing that our football dreams are still alive.

For Kenyans, football is more than just a sport; it's an emotional rollercoaster, a social glue, and a way to forget our everyday struggles for 90 minutes. In those moments, whether we're watching Manchester United blow another lead or Harambee Stars squeeze out a narrow win, we're all united in passion, frustration, and hope. And, let's be honest, a bit of delusion about next year being "our year."

The Power of Culture: Music, Dance, and the Kenyan Soul

If sports unite us physically, **Kenyan culture** unites us spiritually and emotionally. Whether it's through music, dance, or traditional art, Kenya's rich cultural heritage is the beating heart of the nation. And if you think Kenyans are passionate about sports, wait until you see us on the dance floor.

Kenya is home to **over 40 tribes**, each with its own unique traditions, songs, dances, and rituals. From the rhythmic **Isukuti drums of the Luhya** to the iconic **Adumu (jumping dance) of the Maasai**, Kenyan culture is as diverse as it is vibrant. But what's truly magical is how these different cultures come together to form a **shared national identity**. You don't have to be Maasai to appreciate their music, and you don't have to be Kikuyu to enjoy the captivating sounds of **Mugithi**.

Take, for instance, the way Kenyan music has evolved over the years. From the golden age of **Benga music** in the

1960s and '70s to the modern-day beats of **Gengetone**, music has always been a way for Kenyans to express their joy, pain, and hope. It's impossible to sit still when a classic **Daudi Kabaka** track comes on, just as it's impossible to resist the infectious energy of a **Sauti Sol** performance. Kenyan music cuts across generations, and it's not uncommon to see grandmothers and their grandchildren dancing together to the same tune—one generation jiving to **Benga**, while the other grooves to **Octopizzo**.

And then there's **Kenyan dance**, where even the most reserved individuals suddenly discover they have rhythm. Whether it's the traditional **Taarab dances of the Swahili coast** or the popular **Ohangla beats of the Luo**, dance is an integral part of Kenyan culture. We dance at weddings, funerals, political rallies, and even church services. In fact, a Kenyan event isn't truly successful unless someone starts dancing—usually the one uncle who swears he "used to be a professional."
Cultural festivals like **Kenya Music Festival** and **Carnival Nairobi** bring people from all corners of the country together, showcasing our diversity while reminding us of our shared heritage. And in recent years, Kenyan culture has been making waves internationally, with our musicians, artists, and dancers performing on global stages. Whether it's **Maasai beadwork on the runway** in Paris or a **Kenyan band performing at Coachella**, our culture has become a source of national pride, uniting us not just as Kenyans, but as global citizens.
The Role of Sports and Culture in National Unity

So why do sports and culture matter so much in the quest for national unity? Because **they provide a platform where tribal, political, and economic divides melt away**. When we're cheering on Eliud Kipchoge as he breaks another world record, it doesn't matter whether you're Kikuyu, Luo, Kalenjin, or Luhya. When you're dancing to the beats of **Nyashinski** or **Femi One**, no one asks what political party you support. In these moments, we are simply Kenyans, united in joy, celebration, and a shared sense of pride.

Sports and culture also serve as a **mirror for our aspirations**. They remind us of what we can achieve when we come together. They show us that despite our differences, we are one people, striving for excellence, creativity, and innovation. In many ways, sports and culture reflect the best of who we are as a nation—they are symbols of our resilience, our resourcefulness, and our ability to adapt and thrive.

But perhaps most importantly, sports and culture provide us with moments of **laughter and lightness** in an otherwise challenging world. Whether we're cracking jokes about Harambee Stars' latest performance or dancing off the stress of everyday life at a family gathering, these shared experiences bring us closer together. And in a country as dynamic and diverse as Kenya, that's no small feat.

Conclusion: The Marathon Continues, and the Beat Goes On

As we look ahead to the future of Kenya, it's clear that **sports and culture will continue to play a vital role in shaping our national identity and uniting us as a people.** Whether it's through the triumphs of our athletes, the beats of our music, or the rhythms of our traditional dances, sports and culture offer us a way to connect with each other, to celebrate our shared heritage, and to dream of a brighter, more unified Kenya.

So, as we continue to cheer for our runners, to dance to our favorite tunes, and to argue about football (because let's face it, that's not going to stop anytime soon), let's remember the power of sports and culture to bring us together. **The marathon continues, and the beat goes on.** Let's keep running, keep dancing, and keep building a Kenya we can all be proud of—together.

Reviving the Spirit of Ubuntu – Strengthening Family and Community Bonds

Ladies and gentlemen, boys and girls, buckle up for a wild, hilarious, and slightly emotional ride through the magic that is **Ubuntu**—that ancient African concept that has the power to heal nations, bring people together, and possibly even save you from those awkward family reunions where everyone asks, "So, when are you getting married?" We're diving into the deep end of **family and community bonds**—the very glue that holds societies together. In Kenya, as in much of Africa, there's an unspoken understanding that we're all connected. But somewhere along the line, we started drifting apart, like long-lost cousins who only see each other during election campaigns.

What happened to the good old days when family meant more than just people you shared a surname with, and community wasn't just your WhatsApp group? It's time to revive the **spirit of Ubuntu**, rediscover the magic of community, and recognize that national progress starts from the smallest social unit: the family. Ready to laugh, cry, and maybe even call that auntie you've been avoiding? Let's dive in!

Rediscovering the Role of Family and Community in Shaping Culture

Let's take a trip down memory lane, back to when life was simpler. There were no TikToks to make you feel out of touch with pop culture, and no 24-hour news cycles to remind you that the world is a mess. Back then, your **family** and your **community** were everything. The family wasn't just a group of people living under one roof—it was your first school, your emotional support system, and your social safety net. **Parents, grandparents, uncles, and aunties** all played their part in teaching children the values of respect, hard work, and (most importantly) how to dodge a well-aimed slipper if you messed up.

But the real magic happened in the **community**. In traditional Kenyan society, everyone had a role to play, and there was no such thing as "not my problem." If your neighbor's cow went missing, the whole village would be out looking for it. If a child misbehaved, the local elder would dish out wisdom (and maybe a light scolding), because back then, **every child belonged to the community**. In short, people actually cared about each other.

Fast forward to today, and things have gotten a bit... weird. We're all busy chasing success, glued to our phones, and "following" each other on social media but forgetting to check in on our real-life neighbors. Families are shrinking, and communities are becoming more fragmented. But here's the kicker: **we need each other now more than ever**. In a world that's increasingly isolating, the power of family and community isn't just nostalgic—it's essential for survival.

The Power of Mutual Aid and Collective Responsibility

Now, let's talk about the magic of **mutual aid** and **collective responsibility**—two concepts that have the power to turn any tough situation into a slightly less tough one. Remember the phrase, "It takes a village to raise a child"? Well, it also takes a village to build a nation, run a household, and occasionally make it through a Kenyan wedding without losing your mind over the guest list drama.

Mutual aid isn't a new concept in Kenya. Long before the invention of government welfare programs (or those long lines at NHIF offices), communities had their own version of **social security**. It was called **harambee**, which, for those unfamiliar, is basically a call to collective action. Whether it was building a school, fixing a road, or raising funds for a medical emergency, **harambee** was how Kenyans got things done. Everyone chipped in—whether with money, time, or labor—and the job got done because it was for the good of everyone. No government official needed to show up with a ribbon-cutting ceremony.

And here's the hilarious part: harambee was so successful that it became a verb. "We harambeed that thing" is something you might hear if you ask how a project got funded. It's a classic case of "many hands make light work," but in this case, it's "many hands make that school/library/hospital happen, and we're not waiting for the government to figure it out."

Now, **collective responsibility** is the sibling of mutual aid. It's the idea that we all share the burden of making things better. It means we don't just sit back and complain about the potholes on our street or the dilapidated classroom at the local school—we do something about it. Collective responsibility is what turns ordinary people into extraordinary change-makers, and if we could just bottle that spirit and sprinkle it across Kenya, we'd be unstoppable.

Lessons from Kenya's Past on the Importance of Community Unity

Let's get a little sentimental for a moment, shall we? **Kenya's history** is full of beautiful moments of

community unity that remind us of what we're capable of when we come together. In the early days of independence, Kenya was built on the spirit of **togetherness**. Remember the famous motto, "Uhuru na Kazi" (Freedom and Work)? That wasn't just a catchy phrase—it was a call to action. People rolled up their sleeves and got to work, not just for themselves but for their neighbors, their villages, and their country.

One of the most iconic examples of this is the **Mau Mau movement**, where ordinary Kenyans fought against colonialism not as individuals, but as a collective. These freedom fighters were unified by a common cause, and they relied on each other for survival. They shared food, resources, and intelligence because they knew that their success depended on their unity. It was **community in its purest form**—people working together for a better future. Even after independence, communities continued to band together for the common good. The **Green Belt Movement**, founded by Wangari Maathai, is a perfect example. It wasn't just about planting trees—it was about empowering communities to take control of their environment and their future. Women came together, shared knowledge, and fought for their right to a healthy, sustainable environment. They didn't wait for politicians to act—they took matters into their own hands, and in doing so, they changed the course of Kenyan history.

These stories from our past remind us that Kenya's strength has always come from **unity**. Whether it was fighting for independence, advocating for environmental justice, or building schools through harambee, we've always been at our best when we've worked together. The challenge now is to bring that spirit into the present—and into the future.

How Strong Social Fabric Can Support National Progress

Alright, now let's get to the juicy part—**how strong family and community bonds can lead to national progress**. If you're wondering how your family barbecues and neighborhood watch meetings could possibly contribute to Kenya's development, prepare to be enlightened.

First off, **strong families** are the foundation of a strong nation. Think about it: families are where we learn our values, our work ethic, and our sense of responsibility. If you grew up in a Kenyan household, you know the drill. You probably learned how to share your food (even when you didn't want to), how to take care of younger siblings, and how to navigate the treacherous waters of extended family politics. These are life skills that translate directly into how we function as a society.

When families are strong, they raise individuals who are responsible, compassionate, and committed to the greater good. And when individuals are strong, **communities** thrive. A strong community is one where people look out for each other, where neighbors support each other in times of need, and where everyone feels a sense of belonging. And when communities thrive, the nation benefits. It's a **domino effect**—happy families lead to healthy communities, which lead to a prosperous nation.

But it's not just about the feel-good vibes. **Strong social fabric** can have a tangible impact on economic development. When people trust each other and work together, they're more likely to invest in local businesses, support community initiatives, and create opportunities for growth. In fact, research shows that countries with strong community ties tend to have **higher levels of economic**

development and **lower levels of inequality**. So, if we want Kenya to be a thriving, prosperous nation, we need to start by strengthening the bonds between families and communities.

Practical Steps to Strengthen Family and Community Bonds

Now that we've established the importance of **family and community**, let's get practical. How do we go about strengthening these bonds in a world that seems designed to pull us apart? Here are a few ideas:

1. Bring Back Family Dinners
In today's fast-paced world, family dinners have become a rare occurrence. But there's something magical about sitting down together, sharing a meal, and talking about your day. It's a simple way to **reconnect**, build relationships, and reinforce the importance of family.

2. Organize Community Events
Whether it's a clean-up drive, a local sports tournament, or a cultural celebration, community events are a great way to bring people together. They provide an opportunity to **bond**, share ideas, and work together for the common good.

3. Support Local Businesses
One of the best ways to strengthen your community is by **supporting local businesses**. When you shop locally, you're not just getting a great product or service—you're also helping to create jobs and keep money circulating within the community.

4. Get Involved in Your Neighborhood

Whether it's joining a neighborhood association, volunteering at a local school, or just checking in on your elderly neighbor, getting involved in your community is one of the most effective ways to strengthen social bonds. When people feel connected to their community, they're more likely to take responsibility for its well-being.

5. Teach the Next Generation

Pass on the values of **Ubuntu** to the younger generation. Teach children the importance of kindness, responsibility, and collective action. They're the future of Kenya, and it's up to us to equip them with the tools they need to build a better nation.

Conclusion: Ubuntu for a Stronger Kenya

So, what's the moral of the story? **Ubuntu**—the idea that "I am because we are"—isn't just a nice sentiment. It's the foundation of a strong, thriving society. When we strengthen family and community bonds, we create a Kenya that is united, resilient, and capable of achieving greatness.

Our past has shown us that when we work together, we can overcome any obstacle. Our present challenges us to **rebuild the social fabric** that has frayed over time. And our future depends on the choices we make today—whether we choose to stand together or continue drifting apart.

So, let's revive the spirit of Ubuntu. Let's reconnect with our families, strengthen our communities, and work together to build a Kenya where everyone belongs, and everyone thrives.

And who knows? Maybe, just maybe, we'll make those awkward family reunions a little more bearable. **Now that's progress.**

The Role of Religion and Ethics – Guiding Morality and Social Cohesion

In Kenya, religion is a big deal. It's the thread that weaves through the fabric of everyday life, shaping everything from politics to family gatherings, and, of course, weddings. It's so significant that you're never really surprised when a politician opens a rally with a prayer, or when your neighbor asks for a moment of silent reflection before offering you tea (even if it's just three cups of sugar stirred into hot water). Religion is everywhere, from the songs you hear in matatus, to the billboards proclaiming, "JESUS IS LORD," to that one friend who insists on sending you daily Bible verses on WhatsApp.

But religion in Kenya isn't just about Sunday services and mosque visits. It's about the deeper role it plays in shaping moral values, fostering social cohesion, and promoting peace across a country known for its diversity—both in people and beliefs. Religion provides a moral compass for millions, while also serving as a powerful tool for uniting communities that might otherwise be divided by politics, ethnicity, or geography.

In this chapter, we'll explore the sensational, sometimes hilarious, and often heartwarming world of religion in Kenya. We'll reflect on how religious institutions have become the unofficial moral police (without the actual police part), how they've helped keep the peace in turbulent times, and why you should never underestimate the power of a church choir concert to bring people together.

A Nation of Many Faiths: The Kenyan Religious Melting Pot

To truly appreciate the role of religion in Kenya, you need to understand just how diverse the religious landscape is. Kenya is a melting pot of faiths, with Christianity, Islam, traditional African religions, Hinduism, and even the occasional atheist all thrown into the mix. It's not uncommon for one family to have members attending different churches on Sunday mornings, mosques on Friday afternoons, and perhaps even a traditional blessing ceremony thrown in for good measure. In many ways, Kenya's religious diversity reflects the country's broader ethnic and cultural diversity, and for the most part, everyone gets along just fine.

Christianity is the dominant religion, making up roughly 85% of the population. From the grandiose cathedrals in Nairobi to the humble churches in rural villages, Christianity has a deep-rooted influence on Kenyan life. Then there's Islam, practiced by about 11% of the population, especially along the coast and in parts of northern Kenya. Mosques with their beautiful minarets dot cities like Mombasa, where the call to prayer can be heard echoing across the ocean breeze. Meanwhile, traditional African religions still play a role in the lives of many, often blended with other faiths in a way that's uniquely Kenyan.

This religious diversity isn't just something we tolerate— it's something we celebrate. Take, for example, the way Kenyans mark public holidays. We've got Christmas and Easter, Eid al-Fitr and Eid al-Adha, all sharing space on the national calendar. It's like one long, inclusive party, where everyone's invited, and no one leaves hungry. Sure, there are some differences (like how Christians and Muslims don't quite agree on the best way to fast), but overall, religion in Kenya serves as a powerful unifying force in a country that's no stranger to division.

Sunday Morning Madness: Where Religion Meets Kenyan Hustle

If you want to see religion in action in Kenya, just step into a church on Sunday morning. Or better yet, try to get through the traffic on a Sunday morning. Nairobi transforms into a gridlock of cars packed with well-dressed families heading to worship. And let me tell you, Kenyans don't take their Sunday best lightly. It's almost like a fashion show, with people stepping out in crisp suits, colorful dresses, and hats that defy gravity.

Once inside the church, it's an experience like no other. There's singing, dancing, shouting, and sometimes, impromptu sermons delivered by the elderly church auntie who just *had* to tell you about the vision she had last night. There's a vibrant energy that you won't find anywhere else, and if you're lucky, you might even get to witness a church fundraiser, where congregants bid on everything from Bibles to cows (yes, cows).

But beyond the pageantry, the real power of religion is in the sense of community it fosters. Churches, mosques, and temples are more than just places of worship—they're hubs of social cohesion. They're where people come together to share their joys and sorrows, to support each other in times of need, and to work toward the common good. In rural Kenya, a local church might double as a community center, offering everything from free health clinics to farming advice. In urban areas, mosques organize charity drives and distribute food to the less fortunate. Religious institutions in Kenya don't just preach—they practice, and the results are often life-changing.
And then there's the undeniable fact that religion can be a form of comic relief in an otherwise serious world.
Kenyans have a great sense of humor about their religious

practices. There are countless jokes about long-winded sermons that seem to last forever, or about the pastor who asks for "just one more offering" after the fifth collection plate has already been passed around. And let's not forget the *prayer warrior* auntie who insists on sprinkling holy water on everything from your lunch to your car engine, just to be safe.

Ethics and the Moral Compass: Religion as Kenya's Unofficial Regulator

For better or worse, religion in Kenya has also taken on the role of moral gatekeeper. Religious leaders often act as the nation's unofficial regulators, stepping in when they feel the country is veering off track. Whether it's calling out corruption in government, campaigning against immoral behavior (like gambling or alcohol abuse), or providing guidance on social issues, Kenya's religious leaders are never shy about voicing their opinions—and sometimes, their opinions are hard to ignore.

Take, for instance, the ongoing battle between religious institutions and the Kenyan government over issues like same-sex relationships and reproductive rights. In a country where conservatism runs deep, religious leaders have been vocal opponents of policies that they believe go against the moral fabric of society. This has sparked plenty of debate, particularly among younger Kenyans, many of whom are more progressive and believe that personal freedoms should trump religious doctrine.

And while the clash between religion and modernity can sometimes feel like a tug-of-war, it's also a testament to the important role religion plays in shaping ethical discourse in Kenya. Religious leaders often act as mediators during times of crisis, offering moral guidance and promoting peace when tensions run high. During the post-election violence in 2007-2008, for example, religious figures were at the forefront of efforts to heal divisions and encourage reconciliation, organizing interfaith dialogues and praying for peace across the country.

But let's not get too serious—Kenya's moral compass also comes with its fair share of irony and humor. How many times have you seen a Kenyan politician accused of corruption stand at a pulpit on Sunday, asking for prayers while simultaneously dodging allegations of embezzling public funds? It's like watching a soap opera, but with more hymns. And don't get us started on the trend of megachurch pastors who seem to have a direct line to God's wallet, raising eyebrows with their lavish lifestyles while preaching humility from the pulpit. It's a delicate balance, and while Kenyans may joke about it, religion remains a crucial guide for ethics in the country.

Religious Cohesion: When Different Faiths Share the Same Table

One of the most remarkable aspects of religion in Kenya is how well different faiths coexist. Despite being a country with a complex mix of ethnic, cultural, and religious identities, Kenya has largely avoided the kind of sectarian violence that has plagued other parts of the world. This is no small feat, especially considering how closely religion is tied to personal and community identity.

The secret to Kenya's religious harmony? A strong emphasis on interfaith dialogue and mutual respect. It's not uncommon to see Muslims, Christians, and followers of traditional African religions living side by side in peace, attending each other's weddings and funerals, and joining forces during community projects. The rise of interfaith organizations has helped promote understanding between different religious groups, and during times of crisis, religious leaders often come together to promote unity and peace.

Take, for example, the **Inter-Religious Council of Kenya**, a body that brings together religious leaders from across the spectrum to address issues of national concern. Whether it's promoting peace during election periods, addressing the challenges of radicalization, or calling for transparency in government, the council's work highlights how religion can be a force for good, even in a country with diverse beliefs.

But don't think for a second that Kenya's interfaith relations are all solemn and serious. If you've ever attended a joint Christian-Muslim wedding, you know that it's the perfect blend of cultures, traditions, and yes, food. While the bride and groom might spend hours figuring out how to incorporate both faiths into the ceremony, the guests are usually more concerned with whether there'll be enough biryani to go around. And when everyone's stuffed full of food and good vibes, it's hard to remember why people fight over religion in the first place.

Religion and Politics: When Preachers and Politicians Collide

Finally, we'd be remiss if we didn't mention the somewhat complicated relationship between religion and politics in Kenya. It's no secret that Kenyan politicians love to lean on religious institutions for support—after all, there's nothing like a well-timed Bible verse to rally the masses. Whether they're attending Sunday services, participating in iftar

meals during Ramadan, or showing up at a religious event
for some good old-fashioned PR, Kenyan politicians are
well aware of the influence religious leaders have over their
congregations.

But the relationship goes both ways. Religious leaders
aren't afraid to speak out on political matters, and when
they do, people listen. From criticizing government
corruption to endorsing candidates who align with their
values, religious institutions often wield significant
political power. Sometimes, this influence is used for
good—like when religious leaders advocate for peace and
reconciliation during election periods. Other times, it can
be a double-edged sword, particularly when certain
religious leaders use their platforms to stoke political
tensions or spread misinformation.

Still, the intersection of religion and politics in Kenya is
often ripe for humor. You'll often hear jokes about
politicians who suddenly become devoutly religious right
before elections, only to mysteriously disappear from
church pews once the votes are counted. Or the sight of a
politician switching from quoting Bible verses to quoting
economic statistics in the same breath, trying to win over
every last voter. In Kenya, religion and politics are so
intertwined that it's sometimes hard to tell where one ends
and the other begins.

Conclusion: Religion as a Guiding Light for Kenya's Future

Religion and ethics have always played a vital role in
shaping Kenya's moral compass, fostering social cohesion,
and promoting peace across its diverse communities. From
the bustling churches of Nairobi to the peaceful mosques

along the coast, religion provides a sense of unity in a country where divisions—ethnic, political, or otherwise—could easily tear people apart.

As Kenya continues to evolve, the role of religious institutions in guiding morality and promoting social cohesion will remain critical. Whether it's calling out corruption, advocating for peace, or simply providing a space for communities to come together, religion is more than just a private matter—it's a public force for good. And while we may laugh about the quirks of Kenyan religious life, from the never-ending sermons to the all-too-familiar sight of politicians praying for forgiveness, there's no denying the power of faith to shape the nation's future.

So here's to Kenya's religious leaders, moral gatekeepers, and everyday believers who keep the country on course, one prayer at a time. In a world that's constantly changing, they provide a steady hand, guiding Kenya toward a future that's not just prosperous, but ethical, peaceful, and united. And if we can have a few good laughs along the way—well, that's just divine intervention at work.

KEY POINTS AND SUMMARY

Tribalism as a Barrier: Tribalism divides Kenya, stirs conflicts, and hinders progress.

Historical Roots: Colonialism deepened ethnic divides through favoritism and "divide and rule" policies.

Diversity as Strength: Kenya's 42 tribes can be a source of creativity, resilience, and innovation when embraced.

Inter-Ethnic Collaboration: Focus on working together in politics, business, and community projects to foster unity.

Role of Media, Schools, and Leaders: Media should highlight unity, schools can teach cooperation, and leaders must promote inclusion.

A Unified Kenya: Overcoming tribalism can build a stronger, united nation.

Sports and Culture Unite: Sports and culture transcend tribal, political, and economic divides, uniting Kenyans in pride and shared heritage.

Kenya's Running Legacy: Known for world-class marathoners, running symbolizes Kenyan resilience and determination.

Football Passion: Football is Kenya's favorite sport, especially the EPL, despite the national team's struggles, fostering emotional investment.

Cultural Diversity: Kenya's 40+ tribes contribute unique traditions, music, and dance, uniting the nation through shared cultural experiences.

National Unity: Sports and culture offer platforms where differences dissolve, reflecting Kenya's resilience and unity while offering moments of joy and pride.

Ubuntu's Power: Emphasizes the African concept of Ubuntu—community, togetherness, and mutual aid—as crucial for healing and uniting society.

Importance of Family and Community: Strong family and community bonds are essential for societal well-being, teaching values like respect, hard work, and responsibility.

Collective Action: Concepts like *harambee* (mutual aid) and collective responsibility strengthen communities and drive national progress.

Lessons from the Past: Kenya's history shows unity, like the Mau Mau movement and the Green Belt Movement, as key to overcoming challenges.

Practical Steps: Encourages actions like family dinners, community events, and teaching the values of Ubuntu to strengthen bonds.

Religion's Influence in Kenya: Religion is integral to Kenyan life, shaping values, politics, and social gatherings.

Diverse Religious Landscape: Kenya is home to Christianity, Islam, traditional African religions, and more, fostering interfaith harmony.

Religion and Social Cohesion: Religious institutions unite communities, offering moral guidance and practical support like charity and healthcare.

Ethics and Moral Compass: Religious leaders play a key role in guiding ethical discourse, often challenging government corruption.

Interfaith Unity: Different faiths coexist peacefully, promoting mutual respect and interfaith dialogue.

Religion and Politics: Religious influence is significant in politics, shaping political campaigns and public opinion.

Diaspora Contributions – Tapping into Global Kenyan Potential

The Kenyan diaspora is like the distant cousin who left for America or Europe, and now, every time they visit, they're loaded with gifts, tales of foreign lands, and a very noticeable new accent. You know the type—once they've been in the US for a few months, they return with a twang, asking you where the "restroom" is instead of the "choo," and suddenly referring to ugali as "cornmeal." But behind the amusing stories of newfound pronunciations and struggles with winter is a critical force: the Kenyan diaspora is a powerhouse, and its potential to contribute to Kenya's development is nothing short of extraordinary.

Picture this: a Kenyan living in Texas who, while flipping burgers at a fast-food joint to pay the bills, is also masterminding the next big thing in agribusiness back home. Or a Kenyan in London who spends weekends networking with high-profile executives and weekdays running a business consultancy that helps young Kenyan entrepreneurs access global markets. This is the story of the diaspora—living in two worlds, juggling cultures, and finding ways to give back to the motherland in ways that are both hilarious and profoundly impactful.

Let's dive into the world of the Kenyan diaspora, where remittances flow faster than an M-Pesa transaction, knowledge transfer is the new currency, and global networks are the golden goose that could propel Kenya to new heights. Hold on tight—this is going to be a wild, funny, and eye-opening ride.

The Great Kenyan Escape: Chasing Dreams, Dollars, and Winter Jackets

The first step to understanding the power of the Kenyan diaspora is knowing how it all began. Kenyans have been migrating to foreign lands for decades, chasing dreams of better opportunities, higher education, and, of course, those elusive dollars. The moment a Kenyan secures a visa to the UK, US, or Australia, they immediately become a local hero. Family members gather around to send them off like they're about to board a spaceship to Mars. Aunties hand over envelopes stuffed with lists of demands, everything from flat-screen TVs to a new wardrobe (because apparently, clothes in Kenya aren't good enough). And the departing Kenyan promises to return soon, usually adding, *"I'll send something back from abroad!"*

Fast forward six months, and our Kenyan-in-the-diaspora is knee-deep in student loans or working double shifts, discovering that life abroad isn't exactly the paradise advertised in movies. Winter has hit, they're wrapped in seven layers of clothing, and the closest thing they've seen to a dollar is a receipt for overpriced coffee. Yet, despite these struggles, they send money home regularly, providing vital financial support to families and communities back in Kenya.

This, my friends, is the magic of remittances. Kenyans in the diaspora sent a staggering $3.7 billion home in 2021 alone, making remittances one of Kenya's largest sources of foreign income, second only to tea and coffee. If remittances were a person, they'd be the wealthy uncle at family gatherings, casually handing out 1,000-shilling notes while reminding everyone that they single-handedly saved the economy.

But sending money home isn't just about supporting loved ones—it's an investment in Kenya's development. Those remittances pay for school fees, build homes, and fund small businesses. It's like having a secret economic engine that operates across borders, quietly pumping life into the

Kenyan economy while diaspora Kenyans grumble about how expensive rent is in New York.

Remittances: When a Simple "Hustle" Becomes a Lifeline

Let's talk more about remittances—the MVPs of diaspora contributions. These little financial lifelines are the unsung heroes of Kenya's development story. Picture this: your cousin abroad calls you, slightly exasperated, and says, *"I've sent something small via M-Pesa, just a little help."* A few minutes later, your phone buzzes with the equivalent of a small fortune. You look at the amount and think, *"This is 'small?' If this is small, I can't wait to see what big looks like!"*

The beauty of remittances is that they have a ripple effect. The money sent back home doesn't just sit in someone's bank account. It's used to start businesses, pay off loans, and even fund community projects. You know that fancy boda boda station down the road? Chances are it was funded by a remittance from someone's cousin living in Dubai. And the maize mill that's feeding half the village? It's probably thanks to your auntie who's been working as a nurse in Canada for the past five years.

Remittances have single-handedly turned the Kenyan diaspora into a collective superhero squad, each member fighting the good fight against poverty and underdevelopment with their monthly money transfers. What's even more remarkable is how creative Kenyans have become in turning these funds into sustainable businesses. Diaspora money is often used to launch ventures in agriculture, construction, and retail, proving that even while living thousands of miles away, Kenyans remain deeply connected to their roots.

But it's not all smooth sailing. Diaspora Kenyans often find themselves in the hilarious position of being the family ATM. You know the drill: a relative you haven't spoken to in years suddenly calls you out of the blue, reminding you that you share the same ancestors, and oh, by the way, they need help buying a plot of land. It's as if living abroad automatically makes you a millionaire, despite the fact that you're surviving on instant noodles and energy drinks. The struggles are real, but so is the impact.

Knowledge Transfer: Bringing the World to Kenya, One Brain at a Time

While remittances are the most visible contribution from the diaspora, they're not the only way Kenyans abroad are giving back. Let's talk about knowledge transfer, a concept that's rapidly becoming one of the most exciting developments in the diaspora world. Think of it as Kenyans exporting their brains to the world, learning everything they can, and then bringing that knowledge back home. It's like a Trojan Horse, but instead of soldiers, it's filled with cutting-edge skills and groundbreaking ideas.

Imagine a Kenyan software engineer working for a top tech company in Silicon Valley. By day, they're developing apps that could change the world, and by night, they're mentoring young Kenyan developers online, teaching them how to code and compete in the global market. Or picture a Kenyan doctor in Germany who, after mastering advanced medical techniques, regularly flies home to conduct free health camps in rural areas. These are not hypothetical scenarios—they're happening all the time, and they're transforming Kenya in ways we never thought possible.

The beauty of knowledge transfer is that it doesn't require massive sums of money—just dedication and a good internet connection (which, let's face it, can be a challenge in parts of Kenya). The Kenyan diaspora is constantly sharing their expertise through webinars, virtual workshops, and partnerships with local institutions. They're bringing the world to Kenya, one skill at a time, helping to bridge the gap between developed and developing economies.

But knowledge transfer isn't always straightforward. Take, for instance, the Kenyan engineer who tried to introduce robotic farming techniques to his village. The local farmers, who had been using oxen and hoes for decades, stared at him like he had just suggested using magic beans. It took months of persuasion, demonstrations, and probably a few *"But this is how they do it in America!"* conversations before the farmers warmed up to the idea. The result? Increased crop yields and a village that's now the proud owner of a robotic tractor. Progress, albeit with a side of skepticism.

Global Networks: The Diaspora's Secret Superpower

Now, let's talk about the ultimate weapon in the Kenyan diaspora's arsenal: global networks. These connections are like the Swiss Army knife of development tools—they can do just about anything, from helping entrepreneurs secure funding to landing a Kenyan artist a gallery show in Paris. The diaspora has access to a world of resources that would otherwise be out of reach for many back home. They're the bridge between Kenya and the international community, and they're using that bridge to bring in investment, expertise, and opportunities.

Picture this: a Kenyan startup founder who's struggling to raise capital for their groundbreaking fintech app. Enter the diaspora connection—a relative living in London who knows someone who knows someone at a venture capital firm. Suddenly, the startup founder is on a Zoom call with investors in London, New York, and Dubai, pitching their idea to a global audience. Within weeks, they've secured the funding they need, all thanks to a diaspora network that spans continents.

But it's not just about business. The diaspora's global connections are also making waves in culture, politics, and education. Kenyan writers are being published internationally, Kenyan politicians are learning best practices from other democracies, and Kenyan students are getting scholarships to top universities, all because of the diaspora's far-reaching networks. It's like having a Kenyan embassy in every major city around the world, except instead of diplomats, it's everyday Kenyans making moves behind the scenes.

The best part? These networks are growing every day. Diaspora Kenyans are constantly building new connections, whether it's through professional associations, alumni groups, or the ever-popular social media platforms. They're turning LinkedIn into a Kenyan think tank and WhatsApp into a global investment hub. It's diaspora diplomacy at its finest, and it's positioning Kenya as a serious player on the world stage.

The Diaspora's Comic Relief: Navigating the Double Life

Of course, living in the diaspora isn't all about remittances, knowledge transfer, and global networks. There's a hilarious side to it, too—the struggle of navigating a double life. On one hand, you're living in a foreign country, trying to blend in and understand cultural nuances that don't involve nyama choma (grilled meat) and Swahili proverbs. On the other hand, you're still deeply Kenyan, trying to keep up with the latest Nairobi gossip and ward off relatives asking for money every other week.

Diaspora Kenyans are experts in code-switching, switching seamlessly between discussing the stock market in English and debating who makes the best chapati in Swahili. They'll complain about how cold it is in Toronto, and then immediately start planning their next vacation to Mombasa, where the sun is guaranteed. And let's not forget the food cravings—there's nothing quite like trying to explain to a baffled Canadian colleague why you're craving "githeri" (a traditional Kenyan dish of maize and beans) in the middle of a team meeting.

But despite the comedic moments, diaspora Kenyans never forget their roots. They may be thousands of miles away, but their hearts are always back in Kenya, finding ways to contribute, uplift, and transform the country they call home.

Conclusion: From Afar, With Love

The Kenyan diaspora is a force to be reckoned with. They're sending money, sharing knowledge, building networks, and cracking jokes along the way. They're the unsung heroes of Kenya's development story, quietly shaping the nation's future from all corners of the globe.

Whether it's remittances funding a new school, knowledge transfer improving healthcare, or global networks opening doors for young entrepreneurs, the diaspora is proving that you don't have to live in Kenya to love it or to make a difference. They are Kenya's secret weapon—a weapon that's only growing stronger with time.

So, the next time you meet a Kenyan abroad who's talking about their latest business venture while wearing a scarf in 15-degree weather, give them a high five. They're part of the Kenyan dream, working tirelessly to build a better, brighter future for us all—from wherever they may be in the world.

Regional Integration – Kenya's Role in East African and Continental Growth

Imagine a family reunion where everyone shows up, not just with different ideas of how to run things, but with different opinions about what time the reunion should start, who should be in charge of cooking, and whether or not they should even be there. Now, imagine that family reunion happening every year with members who come from vastly different backgrounds, speaking different languages, and arguing about everything from borders to bananas. Congratulations, you've just stepped into the world of regional integration in Africa.

Kenya, like that eager middle child who tries to keep the peace at family gatherings, plays a crucial role in promoting regional cooperation, particularly within the **East African Community (EAC)** and the **African Union (AU)**. From championing free trade agreements to promoting stability and peace, Kenya has become a key player in the drive for regional and continental growth. But as you can imagine, getting a bunch of countries with differing priorities to agree on anything is like herding goats during a downpour: messy, chaotic, and often hilarious.

In this chapter, we'll dive into Kenya's role in regional integration, unpacking its contributions to East African and continental development while exploring the often absurd (and sometimes comical) nature of trying to get an entire region or continent to work together. Spoiler alert: there will be border disputes, diplomatic faux pas, and the occasional argument over who makes the best chapati.

The East African Community (EAC): It's Like a Sibling Rivalry… But With Borders

The **East African Community (EAC)** is made up of six partner states: Kenya, Uganda, Tanzania, Rwanda, Burundi, and South Sudan. If these countries were a family, Kenya would be the overachieving sibling who gets straight As in class and volunteers to help with everything, Tanzania would be the laid-back sibling who prefers to do things at their own pace, Uganda would be the sibling who's always cracking jokes (but occasionally gets into trouble), Rwanda would be the disciplined sibling who insists on following the rules, Burundi would be the quiet one who just wants everyone to get along, and South Sudan—well, South Sudan is the youngest sibling still trying to figure things out.

On paper, the EAC is a regional powerhouse. The idea is simple: bring together these countries, promote free trade, eliminate borders (or at least make them less complicated), and form a common market where goods, services, and people can flow freely. In theory, it's brilliant. In practice, it's like trying to organize a surprise birthday party for someone who already knows about it, but insists on pretending they don't.

Kenya, being one of the largest and most economically advanced countries in the EAC, has played a pivotal role in pushing for deeper integration. Whether it's promoting the **East African Customs Union**, advocating for the **East African Monetary Union**, or supporting the movement towards a **political federation**, Kenya has been front and center, waving the flag for regional unity. And while Kenya's efforts have been commendable, the journey hasn't exactly been smooth sailing.

Take, for example, the time when Tanzania and Kenya got into a bit of a tiff over—wait for it—**bananas**. In 2020, Kenya banned Tanzanian imports of certain agricultural products, including maize, beans, and bananas, citing quality concerns. Tanzania, not one to take things lying down, responded by banning Kenyan goods in retaliation. For a while, it seemed like the entire integration process could be derailed by a bunch of bananas (because of course). Thankfully, cooler heads prevailed, and the two countries eventually came to an agreement. But if this sounds like a sibling rivalry gone wrong, it's because, well, it kind of is.

Despite the occasional spat, the EAC has achieved remarkable progress in many areas. Cross-border trade has increased significantly, regional infrastructure projects like the **Northern Corridor** (which connects the port of Mombasa to landlocked countries like Uganda, Rwanda, and South Sudan) have improved transport and logistics, and regional cooperation in sectors like tourism and energy has boosted economic growth. And let's not forget the **East African passport**, which allows citizens of member states to travel within the region without needing a visa—talk about convenience!

The African Union (AU): A Continental Family Gathering (with a Lot of Speeches)

Now let's zoom out and look at Kenya's role in the **African Union (AU)**, the continental organization tasked with promoting peace, unity, and development across all 55 member states. If the EAC is a sibling rivalry, the AU is a full-blown family reunion with uncles, aunties, cousins, and that one relative who always insists on making a speech at every opportunity.

Kenya has been an active participant in the AU since its inception, pushing for continental integration and development. Kenya has contributed to **AU peacekeeping missions**, provided leadership on issues like climate change and trade, and supported the **African Continental Free Trade Area (AfCFTA)**, a landmark agreement that aims to create a single market for goods and services across the continent.

But as anyone who's ever been to a big African family gathering knows, getting everyone to agree on something can be an exercise in patience. Whether it's coordinating responses to conflicts, negotiating trade agreements, or deciding who gets to sit where at the table, the AU can be a bit like a never-ending conference, with each country bringing its own set of priorities and interests.

Take **AU summits**, for example. These gatherings are notorious for their marathon speeches and diplomatic formalities. Presidents, ministers, and diplomats from all corners of the continent gather to discuss everything from security to sustainable development. And while the speeches are usually filled with grand visions of Africa's future, the reality is often more complicated. There's a famous story about a certain AU summit where a delegate reportedly fell asleep during the keynote address—because let's be honest, even the best speeches can get a little dull after hour three.

But despite the occasional snooze-fest, the AU has made real progress in key areas. The **African Peace and Security Architecture (APSA)** has been crucial in preventing and resolving conflicts across the continent, and initiatives like **Agenda 2063** lay out a long-term vision for Africa's development. Kenya has been a key player in these efforts, often stepping up to mediate in regional conflicts and promote peace and stability.

The African Continental Free Trade Area (AfCFTA): Free Trade, Free Headaches?

Now, let's talk about one of the most ambitious projects the AU has ever undertaken: the **African Continental Free Trade Area (AfCFTA)**. If you've ever tried to organize a massive event with 55 guests who all have different dietary preferences, you'll have some idea of the scale of this undertaking. The AfCFTA aims to create a single market for goods and services across Africa, making it the largest free trade area in the world. It's like a giant African supermarket where you can buy everything from Moroccan dates to South African wine, without having to worry about pesky tariffs or customs delays.

Kenya, of course, is a big fan of the AfCFTA. As one of Africa's leading economies, Kenya stands to benefit immensely from increased trade with other African countries. The idea is simple: by reducing barriers to trade, African countries can trade more with each other, creating jobs, boosting economic growth, and reducing dependence on external markets.

But as with any large-scale project, there are challenges. One of the biggest headaches facing the AfCFTA is, unsurprisingly, logistics. If you've ever tried to import a car from Japan through Mombasa port, you'll know that customs procedures can be as confusing as trying to explain the rules of cricket to someone who's never watched the game. Multiply that by 55 countries, each with their own rules and regulations, and you've got a recipe for potential chaos.

Then there's the issue of infrastructure. For free trade to work, countries need efficient transport networks to move goods across borders. Kenya has been a leader in pushing for regional infrastructure projects like the **Standard Gauge Railway (SGR)**, which connects Mombasa to Nairobi and, eventually, to Uganda and Rwanda. These projects are essential for making AfCFTA a reality, but they're also expensive and time-consuming. Still, if there's one thing Kenyans know how to do, it's hustling—and with the right investment, the dream of a continent-wide free trade area could become a reality.

Kenya as the Diplomatic Powerhouse: Peacekeeping, Mediation, and Conflict Resolution

Kenya's role in regional integration isn't just about trade and infrastructure—it's also about peace and security. Over the years, Kenya has earned a reputation as a diplomatic powerhouse, often stepping in to mediate conflicts and promote stability in East Africa and beyond.

One of the most notable examples of Kenya's diplomatic efforts is its involvement in the **Somalia peace process**. For years, Kenya has hosted peace talks aimed at bringing stability to Somalia, a country that has been plagued by conflict and instability for decades. Kenyan troops have also participated in **African Union Mission in Somalia (AMISOM)**, a peacekeeping mission that has been critical in the fight against extremist groups like **Al-Shabaab**.

But while Kenya's peacekeeping efforts are commendable, they also come with their own set of challenges. Maintaining peace in a region as volatile as East Africa requires constant vigilance, and Kenya's involvement in peacekeeping missions has sometimes drawn criticism from those who argue that it's costly and risky. Still, Kenya remains committed to its role as a peace broker, believing that regional stability is essential for continental growth.

The Hilarious Reality of Regional Politics: Border Disputes and "Friendly" Rivalries

Now, what would regional integration be without a few good-natured rivalries and the occasional border dispute? Kenya's relationships with its neighbors are, shall we say, "complicated." While we're all about unity and cooperation, there's nothing quite like a border dispute to remind everyone that, deep down, we're all still trying to mark our territory.

Take the **Migingo Island** dispute between Kenya and Uganda, for instance. Migingo is a tiny island in Lake Victoria that's smaller than a football field, but for years, it has been the subject of intense debate between the two countries. Despite the island's small size, it's seen as strategically important for fishing rights, and both Kenya and Uganda have laid claim to it. The result? A bizarre and ongoing territorial dispute that has led to everything from diplomatic standoffs to memes poking fun at how both countries are fighting over what is essentially a glorified rock.

Then there's the **Rwanda vs. Kenya** friendly rivalry, particularly when it comes to governance and development. Rwanda, often referred to as the "Singapore of Africa," is known for its efficient government, clean streets, and disciplined citizens. Kenya, on the other hand, is more… let's say "chaotic," but also full of energy and innovation.

The two countries often engage in friendly competition over who's doing better economically, politically, and even in sports. It's all in good fun (mostly), but it's a reminder that even in regional cooperation, a little rivalry isn't a bad thing.

Conclusion: The Future of Regional Integration – Kenya's Role in Leading the Way

Kenya's role in regional and continental integration is undeniable. As a key player in both the **East African Community** and the **African Union**, Kenya has shown time and time again that it's committed to promoting trade, stability, and cooperation across borders. Whether it's pushing for free trade agreements, mediating conflicts, or advocating for regional infrastructure projects, Kenya is at the forefront of the movement to create a more integrated and prosperous Africa.

But regional integration is not without its challenges. From border disputes to logistical headaches, the road to unity is often a bumpy one. Still, Kenya's leadership in these efforts is crucial, and with the right mix of diplomacy, innovation, and good-natured humor, there's no doubt that the dream of a fully integrated East Africa—and eventually Africa—can become a reality.

So, here's to Kenya: the middle child of East Africa, the hustler, the peacemaker, and the ultimate team player. In the grand game of regional integration, Kenya is not just participating—it's leading the charge. And if that means sorting out a few banana-related disputes along the way, so be it.

Immigration and Border Security – Balancing Openness and National Safety

Kenya, the land of safaris, coffee, and an ever-expanding matatu culture, has long prided itself on its hospitality. Whether you're a tourist lost in the winding streets of Nairobi, a refugee seeking safety, or a businessperson looking for new opportunities, Kenya has always had an open-door policy—sometimes so open that a few chickens might wander in too. But with growing challenges around immigration, refugee management, and border security, the country now faces the delicate balancing act of remaining an open and welcoming society while ensuring national safety and security.

You see, managing borders is a bit like managing a party—too many uninvited guests, and things can get messy. But if you turn away everyone at the door, it won't be much of a party either. Kenya, which shares borders with five other countries (and has a coastline teeming with its own set of challenges), must constantly juggle the need to secure its borders while maintaining the spirit of African unity and hospitality.

In this chapter, we'll take a deep dive into the world of Kenyan immigration and border security, complete with tales of sneaky smugglers, overstretched immigration officers, and an occasionally overzealous border wall project. Along the way, we'll examine how Kenya can balance the need for safety and prosperity with its longstanding tradition of openness—while keeping a healthy sense of humor, of course.

The Border Is Not Just a Line: Kenya's Unique Geographical Challenge

Kenya's borders are as diverse as the country itself. To the east, the Indian Ocean forms a natural coastline where dhows still sail, fishermen cast their nets, and traders bustle around Mombasa's historic port. To the north, there's the long, often lawless border with Somalia, where security challenges have kept everyone on their toes for years. To the west, Lake Victoria provides a watery border with Uganda, while the lush highlands mark Kenya's border with Tanzania. And up north, bordering Ethiopia and South Sudan, you've got dry, arid lands where pastoralists and traders cross paths—and occasionally, lines.

With so many neighbors and such a diverse landscape, it's no wonder that managing Kenya's borders is like trying to corral a herd of particularly stubborn goats. Every border comes with its own set of unique challenges, from managing cross-border trade to dealing with insecurity and terrorism threats. One minute, the focus is on the bustling trade routes that keep goods flowing between Kenya and its neighbors, and the next, all eyes are on border security concerns.

And let's not forget the occasional diplomatic kerfuffle that arises over border disputes, like the time Kenya and Uganda got into a minor standoff over the tiny island of **Migingo**. This little patch of land in Lake Victoria is smaller than a football field but sparked a battle of wills between the two countries that included everything from patrol boats to Twitter wars. It's all part of the delicate dance of managing borders in East Africa.

Refugees and Immigration: The World at Kenya's Doorstep

When it comes to immigration, Kenya is no stranger to hosting people from all walks of life. As a regional hub for trade, tourism, and diplomacy, Nairobi has long been a magnet for expatriates, diplomats, and international workers. But immigration in Kenya is about more than just business travelers and tourists—it's also about refugees, who come seeking safety from conflict and persecution in neighboring countries.

Kenya is home to some of the largest refugee camps in the world, including **Dadaab** and **Kakuma**, which have been operating for decades. These camps, initially meant to be temporary shelters for people fleeing war in Somalia, South Sudan, and beyond, have since grown into sprawling settlements that house hundreds of thousands of refugees. And while Kenya has been praised for its hospitality, the reality of managing such a large refugee population is anything but easy.

At its peak, **Dadaab Refugee Complex** housed over half a million refugees, making it one of the largest refugee camps in the world. Managing this population comes with challenges ranging from providing basic services like food and healthcare, to ensuring security, especially with concerns over infiltration by extremist groups like **Al-Shabaab**. But despite the challenges, Kenya continues to keep its doors open—albeit with some trepidation. There's always the balancing act of maintaining national security while upholding international humanitarian obligations.

But here's where things get a bit tricky—and funny, if you have a warped sense of humor like most Kenyans. While the government has periodically announced its intention to close down Dadaab (leading to several international outcries), every time they actually try to do it, it's like a bad breakup that keeps getting postponed. "This is the last time!" they say, but then somehow, the camp stays open. Dadaab has become the "we'll close it next time" story of Kenyan politics.

And then there's the immigration system for non-refugees, which is a whole other ball game. Kenya's immigration services are as bureaucratic as they come, with a level of complexity that would leave even the most seasoned traveler scratching their head. From work permits to residency visas, the system is notorious for delays, lost files, and sometimes inexplicable decisions. One might argue that navigating Kenyan immigration is a rite of passage for anyone brave enough to try living and working in the country. Need a visa extension? You'll likely find yourself queuing in a stuffy office, praying that the immigration officer didn't take an extended tea break right before you got to the front.

But despite the occasional chaos, Kenya remains a popular destination for immigrants, particularly from neighboring countries. Nairobi, with its booming economy and vibrant culture, is a melting pot of nationalities, and you're just as likely to meet a Ugandan entrepreneur setting up shop as you are to meet a British expatriate working in the NGO sector. This diversity is one of Kenya's greatest strengths, contributing to its status as an economic powerhouse in the region.

Border Security: Building Walls, Chasing Smugglers, and the Case of the Floating Fishermen

When it comes to border security, Kenya's challenges range from the serious (terrorism threats and smuggling) to the outright absurd (like that time Somali fishermen allegedly floated across the ocean and were caught with "fishy" cargo). One of the most pressing issues has been securing the long, porous border with Somalia, which has been a hotspot for illegal crossings, smuggling, and infiltration by extremist groups.

In recent years, Kenya's government has ramped up efforts to secure this border, including the controversial construction of a security wall along the Kenya-Somalia border. The wall, dubbed the **Kenya-Somalia Border Security Wall**, is intended to curb the movement of militants from **Al-Shabaab**, who have been responsible for several high-profile attacks in Kenya, including the devastating **Westgate Mall attack** and the **Garissa University massacre**.

Now, walls are a tricky thing. On one hand, they provide a physical barrier to deter illegal crossings. On the other hand, they're not exactly foolproof. And when you're trying to build a wall across rugged terrain with a coastline to boot, things are bound to get complicated. There have been stories of smugglers digging tunnels, fishermen using boats to bypass the wall, and, in one particularly comical case, rumors of people throwing contraband over the wall, only to have it land in the wrong place.

But border security isn't just about walls and checkpoints—it's also about the people working behind the scenes to keep Kenya safe. Border patrol officers, customs agents, and even the Kenya Defense Forces (KDF) play a crucial role in managing the country's borders. And while their work is serious, the stories they tell often have a touch of humor. One border officer, when asked about the most unusual thing he'd ever confiscated, reportedly said, "A live goat stuffed in the back of a Toyota Prius." Because of course, in Kenya, even the most mundane objects can become part of a smuggling operation.

Then there's the issue of human trafficking, which remains a serious concern along Kenya's borders. Unscrupulous traffickers often exploit the desperation of migrants, leading them across borders under dangerous and inhumane conditions. The government, in cooperation with international organizations, has stepped up efforts to crack down on trafficking rings, but it's an ongoing battle that requires constant vigilance.

The Balancing Act: Openness vs. Security
Perhaps the biggest challenge Kenya faces when it comes to immigration and border security is balancing openness with national safety. On the one hand, Kenya prides itself on being a regional leader in trade, diplomacy, and humanitarianism. The country's role as a host for refugees, as well as its thriving tourism industry, means that it benefits from being open to the world.

On the other hand, Kenya cannot afford to ignore the very real security threats it faces, particularly from extremist groups and organized crime syndicates. The threat of terrorism looms large, especially given the proximity to Somalia and the presence of militant groups like Al-Shabaab. Add to this the ongoing challenges of smuggling, human trafficking, and cross-border crime, and it becomes clear that securing Kenya's borders is no easy task.
The government's efforts to strike a balance between openness and security are sometimes met with mixed reactions. While the security wall along the Somalia border is seen by some as a necessary step to curb terrorism, others view it as a heavy-handed approach that could undermine cross-border relations. Similarly, Kenya's decision to host large refugee populations is praised by humanitarian groups but raises concerns about the long-term impact on resources and security.

The trick, of course, is finding a way to protect the country without closing it off. Kenya's future prosperity depends on maintaining strong trade ties with its neighbors, attracting tourists and investors, and continuing to play a leading role in regional diplomacy. At the same time, ensuring the safety of Kenyan citizens is paramount, and this means taking a hard line on issues like smuggling, trafficking, and terrorism.

Conclusion: The Art of Border Management, Kenyan Style

When it comes to immigration and border security, Kenya is walking a tightrope, balancing the need to remain open and welcoming with the imperative to protect its people and borders. From managing sprawling refugee camps to cracking down on cross-border crime, Kenya's approach to border security is as diverse as its landscape. And while the challenges are many, so too are the opportunities.

As Kenya continues to navigate the complex world of immigration and border security, one thing is clear: the country's strength lies in its ability to adapt, innovate, and occasionally, laugh in the face of adversity. Whether it's building walls, repurposing boda bodas as ambulances, or figuring out how to keep goats from being smuggled in the back of a Prius, Kenya's approach to border management is uniquely Kenyan—equal parts resourceful, resilient, and yes, occasionally hilarious.

So here's to Kenya, where borders are more than just lines on a map, and where the balance between openness and security is a challenge we take on with grit, grace, and a healthy dose of humor. After all, what's a border if not a place for a little bit of drama—and a whole lot of opportunity?

Peace and Security – The Foundation of National Stability

If peace is the foundation of national stability, then Kenya is the slightly chaotic but charming family gathering where everyone's trying to get along—most of the time. Picture a family barbecue, where the uncles are loudly debating politics, your aunt is interrogating you about when you're getting married, and there's a cousin somewhere in the background setting off a few harmless fireworks. Everyone knows that if things go sideways, it could get messy fast, but for now, the atmosphere is tense but manageable. That's Kenya: a nation balancing on a tightrope, constantly working to maintain peace while trying not to tip over into conflict.

Peace and security aren't just the absence of violence. In Kenya, peace is that delicate, fragile thing we all cling to, hoping that our neighbors won't wake up one day and decide that today's the day to revisit old land disputes, political grievances, or the eternal battle over who makes the best nyama choma. It's an elaborate dance involving peacebuilding, conflict resolution, and the continuous work of enhancing security systems, all in the hope that we can build a stable nation where we can focus on more important things—like who's playing in the World Cup and why Nairobi traffic is a national disaster.

In this chapter, we'll dive into Kenya's journey toward peace and security. From hilarious tales of conflict resolution that could have been reality TV gold, to the often absurd but effective ways we handle security, we'll explore the role of peacebuilding in keeping Kenya stable. So grab your tea (or something stronger), and let's take a wild, laugh-filled ride through Kenya's peace and security landscape.

The Great Kenyan Peace Summit: When Everyone is a Negotiator

Kenya has an impressive tradition of peacebuilding, where almost everyone seems to have an opinion on how to resolve conflict, from the elders in rural villages to the political pundits on TV. Peacebuilding is so ingrained in our culture that even a family disagreement over land can turn into a mini-summit with half the village in attendance, each person offering a different solution.

Imagine this scenario: two brothers are fighting over a small piece of land. The argument gets heated, and suddenly the local chief, elders, neighbors, and even that one nosy neighbor who wasn't invited, all gather to mediate. Before you know it, tea is being served, everyone's discussing their own land disputes from 20 years ago, and the situation evolves into a full-blown community event. By the time a resolution is reached, no one really remembers what the original conflict was about, but hey—peace has been restored.

It's the same story on a national level. Kenya has a rich history of community-driven peacebuilding efforts, where local leaders step in to mediate conflicts before they escalate into violence. Whether it's cattle rustling in the north or political disagreements in urban centers, the Kenyan approach to peacebuilding often involves a lot of talking, even more tea, and a few well-placed jokes to lighten the mood. The secret sauce to Kenyan conflict resolution? Humor, patience, and the belief that no issue is too big to be solved by a good ol' baraza (community meeting).

But as much as we love to laugh about it, this approach works. Kenya has managed to avoid large-scale civil wars, thanks to grassroots peace efforts that promote dialogue and understanding. Of course, it helps that Kenyans have an endless supply of witty comebacks and one-liners that can diffuse even the most tense situation.

The Post-Election Drama: A National Tradition

In Kenya, elections are like a national sporting event, except instead of cheering for football teams, we're all rooting for political candidates. The excitement is palpable, the stakes are high, and—unfortunately—things can get a little messy. Elections in Kenya are known for their drama, and if you've lived through a few, you know that "peace" becomes a buzzword as soon as the voting booths close. After every election, the entire country holds its breath, waiting to see if the results will be accepted peacefully or if we're about to enter another round of post-election tension. It's like watching the end of a nail-biting football match, except the stakes are much higher, and the consequences of a loss aren't just bruised egos—they can be disastrous for national stability.

Take the 2007-2008 post-election violence, for example. It was a dark period in Kenya's history, where political disagreements spiraled into ethnic tensions and widespread violence. For months, Kenya teetered on the brink of chaos, with communities turning against each other, and the world watching in horror. It was a reminder that peace is fragile, and that once it's broken, it takes a monumental effort to restore.
But out of the ashes of that crisis, Kenya has made significant strides in peacebuilding and conflict resolution. The creation of peace committees, the promotion of national dialogue, and the involvement of international mediators (shoutout to Kofi Annan, the ultimate mediator)

all played a role in restoring calm. And while we still experience post-election tension (with plenty of memes to go with it), the lessons learned from that dark period have shaped how we handle political conflict today.

The Absurdity of Kenyan Security: More Comedic than You'd Expect

Security in Kenya is like that matatu driver who seems to have his own set of rules. One minute it's all fine, and the next, you're wondering how on earth we got here. From the traffic police who wave you over with an exaggerated flourish (only to ask for "kitu kidogo"), to the elaborate but sometimes questionable security measures in malls, Kenya's security landscape can be downright hilarious at times.

Let's start with the airport security checks. You know the drill. You arrive at Jomo Kenyatta International Airport, and before you even get to the terminal, your car has to go through a security check that involves a guard with a mirror-on-a-stick device. What exactly are they looking for? No one really knows, but it's comforting to think that the mirror-on-a-stick is somehow keeping us all safe. Then there's the endless series of metal detectors and bag scans, which we obediently pass through, despite knowing that the security guards are more interested in your phone than in finding anything suspicious.

Or how about the ubiquitous security checks at shopping malls? You pull up to the entrance, roll down your window, and the security guard peers into your back seat as if you've somehow smuggled an entire army into your car. After a quick glance, they wave you through, satisfied that you pose no threat. It's security theatre at its finest, and while it can seem absurd, it's a reminder of Kenya's ongoing efforts to maintain peace in the face of real security threats.

But for all the comedy, Kenya's security forces play a crucial role in keeping the country safe. In recent years, Kenya has faced significant challenges from terrorist groups like Al-Shabaab, which have targeted public spaces, government institutions, and even schools. The 2013 Westgate Mall attack and the 2015 Garissa University attack were stark reminders that peace and security require constant vigilance.

The Kenyan government has since ramped up efforts to combat terrorism, improving intelligence gathering, investing in counter-terrorism training, and working with international partners to strengthen security systems. And while we can laugh about the mirror-on-a-stick, we can't ignore the fact that Kenya's security apparatus has played a key role in preventing further attacks.

The Role of the Kenyan Police: Protectors, Negotiators, and Sometimes, Comedians

Ah, the Kenyan police force—an institution so iconic that it deserves its own comedy series. From their creative traffic management techniques to their uncanny ability to appear exactly when you don't need them, the police are an integral part of Kenya's security landscape. But for all the jokes, they also play a critical role in maintaining peace and security.

Take traffic management, for example. Nairobi's traffic police are like magicians—one moment they're nowhere to be seen, and the next, they're directing traffic with the flair of a conductor leading an orchestra. Of course, their methods can be… unconventional. If you've ever been stuck in Nairobi traffic, you know the chaos that unfolds when a police officer decides to step into the fray. But somehow, against all odds, they manage to keep things moving (most of the time).

And then there's their role in conflict resolution. In rural areas, the police often double as mediators, stepping in to resolve disputes between neighbors, families, and even entire communities. It's not uncommon for a local police officer to be called in to settle a disagreement over grazing land, water access, or livestock theft. And while the process may involve a few laughs (and maybe a few bribes), the end goal is always the same: peace.

But perhaps the funniest (and most frustrating) aspect of the Kenyan police force is their selective presence. Need the police to respond to a burglary? You might be waiting for a while. But accidentally make an illegal U-turn, and suddenly there's a traffic cop materializing out of thin air, ready to issue a fine—or offer you a chance to "negotiate" the matter quietly.

Despite the jokes, the Kenyan police force plays a vital role in maintaining law and order. With proper reforms (and maybe a little more accountability), they have the potential to be even more effective in their peacekeeping efforts.

Sustainable Peace: More Than Just Security

At its core, peace isn't just about having a robust security system or resolving conflicts as they arise. Sustainable peace is about creating a society where everyone feels safe, respected, and included. It's about addressing the root causes of conflict—poverty, inequality, political exclusion—and building systems that promote fairness and justice.

In Kenya, peacebuilding efforts must go beyond putting out fires and focus on creating opportunities for all. This means investing in education, providing economic opportunities, and ensuring that marginalized groups are included in decision-making processes. It's about making sure that every Kenyan, from the bustling streets of Nairobi to the quiet villages of Turkana, feels like they have a stake in the country's future.

And let's not forget about the role of humor. If there's one thing that has helped Kenyans navigate the challenges of peace and security, it's our ability to laugh in the face of adversity. Whether it's cracking jokes about the latest political drama or making light of the endless security checks, humor has always been our way of coping with the chaos around us.

Conclusion: Building a More Peaceful, Secure (and Sometimes Hilarious) Kenya

Peace and security are the foundation of Kenya's future. Without them, all the dreams of development, economic growth, and national unity fall apart. But as we've seen, peacebuilding and security aren't just about serious meetings and somber declarations—they're about the everyday actions we take to resolve conflicts, keep each other safe, and build a society where everyone can thrive. In Kenya, peace is more than a lofty ideal—it's a way of life. It's found in the village baraza where elders settle disputes, in the police officer who directs traffic with a smile (and maybe a bribe), and in the jokes we share as we navigate the complexities of living in a diverse, vibrant nation.

So here's to a more peaceful, secure, and yes, occasionally absurd Kenya. May we continue to laugh, negotiate, and build a country where peace is more than just a word—it's the foundation of everything we do.

KEY POINTS AND SUMMARY

Diaspora's Role: The Kenyan diaspora, though living abroad, plays a crucial role in Kenya's development through remittances, knowledge transfer, and global networks.

Remittances: In 2021, the diaspora sent $3.7 billion back home, funding education, businesses, and community projects.

Knowledge Transfer: Diaspora Kenyans share expertise, helping to improve sectors like agriculture and healthcare.

Global Networks: Diaspora connections open doors for Kenyan entrepreneurs, artists, and students internationally.

Dual Lives: Diaspora Kenyans juggle life abroad with strong connections to their homeland, contributing to Kenya's progress.

Kenya's Leadership Role: Kenya plays a crucial role in promoting regional integration within the East African Community (EAC) and the African Union (AU), advocating for free trade, stability, and infrastructure development.

Challenges of Integration: Regional integration is complex, involving border disputes (e.g., Migingo Island) and trade disagreements (e.g., Kenya-Tanzania banana dispute).

African Continental Free Trade Area (AfCFTA): Kenya supports the AfCFTA, aiming to enhance intra-African trade.

Diplomatic Efforts: Kenya is a key mediator in regional peace processes, such as Somalia's.

Rivalries and Cooperation: Despite challenges, Kenya continues to lead in fostering unity and growth across Africa.

Kenya's Open-Door Policy: Kenya has long welcomed tourists, refugees, and businesspeople, but must balance this with border security.

Geographical Challenges: Kenya's borders with Somalia, Uganda, Tanzania, and its coastline present security and logistical challenges.

Refugee Management: Kenya hosts large refugee camps like Dadaab and Kakuma, but struggles with resource allocation and security risks.

Border Security: Efforts like the Kenya-Somalia wall aim to curb smuggling and terrorism, though challenges persist.

Balancing Act: Kenya must secure its borders while remaining open to trade, tourism, and humanitarian needs.

Kenya's Peacebuilding Culture: From family disputes to national conflicts, peacebuilding in Kenya is deeply ingrained in the culture, often resolved through community-driven efforts and humor.

Post-Election Tensions: Elections can lead to heightened tensions, with notable incidents like the 2007-2008 post-election violence, but Kenya has improved in conflict resolution.

Security Challenges: Kenya faces serious security threats, particularly from terrorism, but also maintains a comical yet effective approach to everyday security.

Sustainable Peace: True peace involves addressing root issues like poverty and inequality, and ensuring inclusive decision-making for long-term stability.

The Power of Civic Engagement – Active Citizenship for a Functional Nation

Ladies and gentlemen, gather around for the main event of the century! The most underrated, yet most powerful force in shaping the future of Kenya: **civic engagement**! That's right, not celebrity endorsements, not political slogans, not even your favorite TV preacher promising "prosperity"— no, the true game-changer is **you**, the everyday citizen. Before you roll your eyes and scroll on, thinking, "Here we go again with another 'power of the people' speech," let me assure you—this is different. This is about **why you matter** more than you think, and how your involvement can turn Kenya from a land of potholes and power outages into a well-oiled machine of efficiency and transparency.

Think about it: have you ever wondered why some countries seem to work like clockwork, while others (ahem, looking at you, Kenya) seem to lurch forward like a matatu with a flat tire? The difference isn't magic or luck—it's **civic engagement**. So buckle up, folks, because we're about to explore how **active citizenship** is the secret sauce to making Kenya a functional nation, one complaint form, one protest sign, and one vote at a time.

The Role of Citizens in Holding Government Accountable

Let's get straight to the point: **governments are like toddlers**. They need constant supervision, clear instructions, and sometimes a good talking-to when they go astray. If you leave a toddler (or a government) unattended for too long, chaos ensues. Suddenly, someone's smeared chocolate all over the walls—or in the case of government, public funds are mysteriously "lost" in someone's offshore bank account.

But here's the kicker: **citizens are the supervisors**. We're the ones responsible for keeping our leaders in check, making sure they don't go on wild shopping sprees with our taxes. Unfortunately, many of us think that accountability begins and ends at the ballot box, as if our job is done the moment we drop that piece of paper into the ballot box and say, "Good luck, leaders! We'll see you in five years!"

Civic engagement is a full-time job, and we're all hired, whether we like it or not. It's about showing up—yes, showing up when your local MP promises to build a road and instead builds a five-story mansion on the coast. It's about asking questions—"What happened to that development fund?" and demanding answers. It's about reminding our leaders that we, the people, are the **employers**, and they're the employees. And guess what? If they're not doing their job, we have the power to fire them. (Okay, it's not as easy as clicking "unfollow" on social media, but you get the point.)

Let me paint you a picture: imagine a Kenya where every citizen felt empowered to hold the government accountable. No more backdoor deals, no more empty promises, no more disappearing billions. Just a functional, transparent government where everyone—from the president to the village chief—knows that the people are watching, listening, and ready to act.

Sounds dreamy, right? Well, that dream starts with **you**.

Promoting Transparency, Participation, and Responsibility in Governance
Now, let's talk about the three magic words: **transparency, participation, and responsibility**. Sounds like a slogan for a futuristic utopia, doesn't it? But here's the truth: these

three principles are the cornerstone of any **functional nation**. Without them, we're stuck in a never-ending loop of corruption, inefficiency, and frustration (you know, like trying to get anything done at a government office).

Transparency

Transparency is simple: it's about being open and honest. If our government isn't as transparent as a glass of clean water (not the brown sludge that sometimes comes out of our taps), then we've got a problem. Transparency means we should know how our taxes are being spent, how decisions are being made, and who is benefitting from them.

But transparency isn't just the government's responsibility—it's ours too. We have to **demand it**. If your local governor's office is claiming they spent Ksh 200 million on a road that still looks like something out of a Mad Max movie, don't just shrug and say, "Ah, that's Kenya for you." Ask questions. File complaints. Use the **Access to Information Act** (yes, that's a thing). The more we demand transparency, the harder it becomes for our leaders to hide behind their fancy titles and vague explanations.

Participation

Let's face it: **most of us are armchair critics**. We love to complain about the government, but when it comes to actually doing something about it, we're suddenly too busy. Civic participation is about getting involved—not just during election season, but every day. It's about attending town hall meetings (yes, they exist), joining community discussions, and voting on local issues. It's about being present, informed, and vocal.

Here's a thought: What if instead of complaining about the lack of services in your area, you joined your local **development committee** and actually influenced how money is spent? What if instead of just grumbling on Twitter, you organized your neighbors and took collective action on that blocked sewer that's been flooding the road for weeks? Participation isn't just a right—it's a duty. And when we all do our part, the government has no choice but to listen.

Responsibility
Finally, let's talk about **responsibility**. As citizens, we have to take ownership of the country's future. It's not just the government's job to make Kenya great—it's ours too. Responsibility means not only holding our leaders accountable but also holding ourselves accountable. It means **paying taxes**, following the law, and contributing to the well-being of our communities.

Responsibility isn't glamorous. It's not the kind of thing that gets you likes on Instagram. But it's the glue that holds everything together. A responsible citizenry is the foundation of a strong, vibrant nation. Without it, all the transparency and participation in the world won't save us.

How Civic Action Leads to Better Public Services

Let's get real: **civic action** isn't just a feel-good buzzword. It actually works. When citizens come together to demand better services, hold leaders accountable, and advocate for change, **things happen**. Roads get built, hospitals get staffed, and public services improve. Don't believe me? Let's look at some real-life examples.

In 2018, a group of residents in **Kibera** (Africa's largest urban slum) decided they'd had enough of the **lack of access to water**. For years, the people of Kibera had been forced to buy water from private vendors at inflated prices because the government had failed to provide proper water infrastructure. So, what did they do? They organized. They petitioned the government, held protests, and even worked with NGOs to build community-based water points. Today, many parts of Kibera have access to **clean, affordable water**—all because the residents took matters into their own hands.

Or how about the **Mukuru Kwa Njenga slum** in Nairobi, where residents came together to form the **Mukuru Community Justice Center**? For years, they were plagued by illegal land grabs, police brutality, and corruption. But instead of just complaining, they took action. They formed committees, educated the community on their rights, and began to hold local authorities accountable. As a result, land grabbing decreased, and the community now has a stronger voice in local governance.

These are just a few examples of how **civic action** leads to better public services. When we stop waiting for the government to magically fix everything and start taking action ourselves, we become the drivers of change. And the best part? We don't need a title or a position of power to make it happen. All we need is a group of dedicated citizens and a willingness to get our hands dirty.

Case Studies of Grassroots Movements in Kenya

Now, let's dive into some of the most inspiring **grassroots movements** that have emerged in Kenya—movements that prove civic engagement isn't just about attending rallies or signing petitions. It's about **transforming communities** from the ground up.

1. The #MyDressMyChoice Movement

In 2014, a video of a woman being assaulted in Nairobi for wearing what some considered "indecent" clothing went viral. The incident sparked outrage across the country and led to the birth of the **#MyDressMyChoice** movement. This grassroots movement, led primarily by women, demanded an end to gender-based violence and the protection of women's rights to dress as they please. What started as a protest in Nairobi quickly gained national attention, forcing the government to take action. Public debates on women's rights intensified, and police were pressured to investigate and arrest the perpetrators. The **#MyDressMyChoice** movement didn't just create awareness—it brought about tangible change. It reminded us that civic action isn't just about political rights—it's about human rights, too.

2. Unga Revolution

Remember the time when the price of **unga (maize flour)** skyrocketed and everyone was panicking because, let's be real, ugali is life? Well, in 2017, a group of activists had had enough. They launched the **Unga Revolution**, a movement that demanded the government take immediate action to lower the price of maize flour, a staple food for millions of Kenyans.

What started as a series of online complaints turned into street protests, with citizens from all walks of life joining in. The pressure on the government was so intense that it had no choice but to **subsidize maize flour**, bringing the price back down to a level people could afford. The Unga Revolution proved that when Kenyans come together to demand change, even something as fundamental as the price of food can be influenced by the power of civic engagement.

3. #StopTheseThieves

Corruption in Kenya is like that bad habit you just can't shake—it's everywhere, and it's persistent. But in 2015, a movement called **#StopTheseThieves** emerged to tackle corruption head-on. Activists and citizens came together to demand accountability from the government, especially in light of massive corruption scandals like the **Eurobond** and **National Youth Service (NYS)** thefts.

Through social media campaigns, protests, and advocacy, the movement raised awareness about the impact of corruption on public services and demanded that those responsible be held accountable. While the fight against corruption is far from over, **#StopTheseThieves** sparked a national conversation that continues to this day. It showed that when citizens band together, even the most entrenched problems can be confronted.

Conclusion: Active Citizenship for a Functional Nation

So, what's the takeaway? **Civic engagement is the secret sauce** to building a functional, transparent, and accountable nation. It's not just about voting or attending the occasional protest—it's about being actively involved in the governance of your country every day. It's about holding leaders accountable, demanding transparency, and participating in the decisions that affect our lives.

When we embrace **active citizenship**, we transform Kenya from a country of passive complainers to a nation of **engaged, empowered individuals** who refuse to accept mediocrity. We can build better roads, schools, and hospitals. We can create a government that serves the people, not the other way around. And we can ensure that the voices of ordinary Kenyans are heard, loud and clear. Remember: **Kenya belongs to all of us**, and it's up to each and every one of us to make it the country we deserve. So, go out there, get involved, and let's build a nation that works for everyone—one civic action at a time.

Now, if you'll excuse me, I've got a town hall meeting to attend.

Media and Information – Shaping National Identity and Accountability

Imagine a Kenyan evening in 1987. The entire family is gathered around a black-and-white TV set, and as the news hour kicks off, the familiar voice of the newscaster booms out, "*Hapa ni habari za Kenya…*" The only choices you have are the national broadcaster and, well, nothing else. The news feels a bit like a sermon, and there's a strict limit on what's covered. Fast-forward to 2024, and the scene is vastly different. Instead of one centralized source of news, we've got thousands—social media platforms, online news outlets, bloggers, YouTubers, and of course, Kenya's very own notorious online warriors, #KOT (Kenyans on Twitter).

Today, the Kenyan media landscape is like a nyama choma buffet: rich, diverse, and maybe a little overwhelming if you don't know where to start. But one thing's for sure: media plays a critical role in shaping national identity, fostering public discourse, and holding leaders accountable. In this chapter, we're diving deep into the sensational, hilarious, and sometimes absurd world of Kenyan media and information.

From the days of tuning into *KBC* (Kenya Broadcasting Corporation) as the only source of information to today's endless stream of WhatsApp forwards and Twitter debates, Kenya's media has undergone a dramatic transformation. And while the evolution of media has made it easier to access information, it has also given rise to a whole new set of challenges, like fake news and, let's face it, a whole lot of conspiracy theories.

But at the heart of it all, one truth remains: the media is a powerful tool that can inform, educate, entertain, and—most importantly—hold leadership accountable. And in Kenya, where leaders sometimes feel like they're playing hide-and-seek with the truth, that accountability is more crucial than ever.

The Media Then and Now: From Government Broadcasts to #KOT

Let's start with a history lesson—Kenya's media wasn't always the wild, unfiltered beast it is today. Back in the day, we had state-controlled media outlets that mostly served to repeat government-sanctioned narratives. You could watch the news, sure, but don't expect much beyond a monotone readout of government achievements, a story about some school winning a netball tournament, and maybe a weather forecast that could be hit or miss (as most weather reports are, to be honest). The media back then was more about broadcasting messages **to** the people, rather than engaging **with** them.

Enter the era of media liberalization. In the 1990s, the Kenyan government relaxed its grip on the airwaves, and soon, independent media houses popped up like matatus in rush-hour traffic. Suddenly, Kenyans had choices—radio stations that played the latest hits, TV channels that reported news without a heavy government filter, and newspapers that dared to ask tough questions. Media outlets like *Nation*, *The Standard*, and *Citizen TV* became household names, each with their own style of reporting and editorial stances. For the first time, the Kenyan public could see a diversity of perspectives.

But things really took off with the rise of the internet and, more importantly, social media. If traditional media is like a well-structured Sunday sermon, social media is like an unsupervised family gathering where everyone's shouting their opinions, no one's listening, and the cousin who just came back from studying abroad is trying to prove they know everything. It's chaotic, yes—but it's also democratizing. Suddenly, everyone has a voice, and that voice can go viral in minutes.

Enter #KOT, arguably one of the most vocal, sharp-witted, and fearless online communities in the world. #KOT is a force of nature, known for their ability to make any issue trend—whether it's calling out corruption or making fun of Ugandan drivers (sorry, Uganda). With a few hashtags and some perfectly timed memes, they can hold politicians accountable, spread awareness, and mobilize support for causes. At the same time, though, #KOT has a tendency to… let's say… take things a bit too far sometimes, with debates spiraling into full-blown online wars over things like which Kenyan county produces the best chapati (let's settle this—it's all delicious, okay?).

But whether it's serious political discourse or light-hearted banter, the point is clear: media, particularly digital media, has become a tool for shaping Kenya's national identity and fostering dialogue. What's more, it has the power to hold leadership accountable in ways that would have been unimaginable just a few decades ago.

Media and Accountability: Exposing the Truth, One Scandal at a Time

There's a popular saying in Kenya: *"Vitu kwa ground ni different."* This essentially means that reality on the ground is often miles apart from the rosy picture some people— often politicians—try to paint. Fortunately, Kenya's media is there to remind us that what we see on TV ads during election campaigns isn't always the whole truth. The media's role as a watchdog is one of its most important functions, especially in a country where politicians sometimes act like they're auditioning for a telenovela with all the drama and plot twists.

Kenyan media has exposed scandals, corruption, and abuses of power that would have otherwise remained hidden. From the infamous "Anglo Leasing" scandal to the more recent "COVID-19 millionaires" scandal, where millions of shillings meant for pandemic relief ended up lining the pockets of a few well-connected individuals, journalists have played a crucial role in bringing these stories to light. It's like watching a soap opera, except with real-life consequences—and far fewer love triangles.

Take the case of investigative journalism in Kenya, led by reporters like *John-Allan Namu* and his team at *Africa Uncensored*. These brave journalists have gone undercover, faced threats, and risked everything to expose the dark underbelly of corruption in Kenya. Their work reminds us that accountability doesn't just happen in Parliament—it happens in the court of public opinion, too. And it's the media that brings the evidence to that court, usually in the form of an exposé that leaves viewers glued to their screens, simultaneously enraged and entertained.

But while traditional media outlets play a crucial role in holding leadership accountable, digital media has opened the door for more voices to join the conversation. Citizen journalism—where regular people report stories or share information—has exploded in popularity, with bloggers, YouTubers, and even TikTok influencers playing the role of investigative journalists. While this democratization of media is empowering, it also comes with its challenges— chief among them being the spread of fake news.

Fake News: The Uninvited Guest at the Media Party

In the age of social media, where everyone with a smartphone can be a reporter, there's a new challenge that wasn't as prevalent in the days of traditional media: fake news. In Kenya, misinformation spreads faster than a WhatsApp forward from your aunt who still believes that Bill Gates is putting microchips in vaccines.

Fake news isn't just annoying—it's dangerous. During the 2017 elections, for example, false reports circulated online, leading to tension and anxiety in an already charged political environment. Misinformation has also played a role in stoking ethnic divisions, spreading fear, and even impacting public health (remember the time people were told that eating garlic could cure COVID-19? Yeah, that happened).

Fortunately, the media and tech-savvy youth are stepping up to tackle this problem. Fact-checking organizations like *PesaCheck* and *Africa Check* have emerged to debunk false stories and set the record straight. These platforms work tirelessly to counter fake news, verifying information and providing the public with accurate data. It's like being the sober friend at a wild party—someone has to make sure things don't spiral out of control.

But while fact-checking is important, the real solution to fake news lies in media literacy. Kenyans need to learn how to critically evaluate the information they consume, to distinguish between credible sources and the guy on Facebook claiming that he's cracked the secret to eternal youth. Schools and universities are increasingly incorporating media literacy into their curricula, teaching young Kenyans how to navigate the often-murky waters of the internet.

Digital Media: Shaping Public Discourse and Democracy

It's hard to overstate the impact of digital media on Kenya's public discourse. Gone are the days when news and political commentary were the exclusive domain of a few well-known journalists or media houses. Today, anyone with a smartphone and an internet connection can weigh in on the issues of the day, from the latest government policy to what happened on the last episode of *Maria*.

Digital media has allowed marginalized voices to be heard, creating spaces for conversations that were previously ignored by mainstream outlets. Issues like LGBTQ+ rights, mental health, and police brutality have gained traction in online forums, thanks in large part to young activists who use social media to amplify their messages. These platforms have become the battlegrounds for social justice, where public pressure can force real change. Just look at the *#EndSARS* movement in Nigeria, which inspired similar activism in Kenya calling for police reform.

Moreover, digital media has been instrumental in fostering democracy in Kenya. During elections, platforms like Twitter and Facebook serve as hubs for voter education, fact-checking, and reporting irregularities. It's not uncommon to see live tweets from polling stations or Facebook posts that expose electoral malpractices in real time. And while these platforms can sometimes be used to spread misinformation, they've also empowered citizens to hold the electoral process accountable.

But it's not just about politics—digital media is shaping national identity in ways we couldn't have predicted. From the global success of Kenyan YouTubers like *Elsa

Majimbo* to the rise of digital artists who use platforms like Instagram to showcase their work, the internet is putting Kenya on the map in new and exciting ways. Kenya is no longer just a country you visit for safaris—it's a hub of creativity, innovation, and cultural exchange, all thanks to the power of digital media.

Conclusion: The Media's Role in Shaping a Nation

At its core, media—whether traditional or digital—plays an irreplaceable role in shaping national identity, fostering accountability, and building a well-informed society. In Kenya, where every news story, meme, and tweet has the potential to spark lively debate, the media is not just a tool for information; it's a mirror reflecting who we are as a nation. It holds up a magnifying glass to our politics, our culture, and our society, showing us the good, the bad, and sometimes, the downright ridiculous.

While Kenya's traditional media continues to provide valuable reporting and investigative journalism, it's the digital revolution that's truly changing the game. Platforms like Twitter, Facebook, Instagram, and YouTube have given everyday citizens the power to contribute to national conversations, to call out injustice, and to push for transparency in once unimaginable ways. Gone are the days when a few elite voices controlled the narrative. Now, it's the people who have the power to shape public discourse, one hashtag at a time.

But with great power comes great responsibility. The rise of digital media has made it easier than ever for misinformation and fake news to spread like wildfire. As much as Kenya's media landscape is empowering, it's also chaotic at times, and it's up to all of us—journalists, bloggers, influencers, and everyday Kenyans—to ensure that the information we share is accurate and responsible. This is where media literacy becomes crucial. Teaching Kenyans, especially the youth, how to critically analyze the news they consume will help build a more informed, resilient society.

When it comes to holding leadership accountable, the media is an essential watchdog. Investigative journalists uncover corruption and malfeasance, while social media movements like #KOT keep leaders on their toes, forcing transparency in an era where nothing stays hidden for long. Kenya's leaders may try to pull a fast one, but they'll quickly find themselves in the crosshairs of a Twitter storm, a trending hashtag, or an exposé on national television. In this sense, the media isn't just a tool for transparency—it's a force for democracy.

However, the most exciting aspect of Kenya's media evolution is how it's shaping our national identity. The stories we tell, the memes we create, the jokes we share online—they all contribute to the larger narrative of who we are as Kenyans. Whether it's celebrating our athletes' success on the world stage, discussing important political issues, or simply debating which county makes the best nyama choma, Kenya's media is a reflection of our culture, our values, and our collective journey as a nation.

In the end, the power of media lies not just in its ability to inform, but in its ability to inspire change. Kenya's future depends on a well-informed public that can hold leaders accountable, demand transparency, and shape the direction of the country. And as long as we have a vibrant, free, and dynamic media landscape—whether it's a national news network or a teenager with a viral TikTok account—there's no limit to what we can achieve.

So here's to Kenya's media, in all its forms—traditional, digital, and everything in between. May it continue to challenge us, entertain us, and push us to be better as a nation. And to all the Kenyans tuning in, tweeting, and tuning out, remember this: you're not just consuming media—you're shaping the future of Kenya with every click, share, and post. Now, that's something worth celebrating.

Culture of Innovation – Fostering Creativity and Problem-Solving

Kenya is a nation that thrives on the idea of "mwanaume ni kujaribu" (a man is defined by trying), which loosely translates to "life is about giving it a shot, even if you have no idea what you're doing." This cultural mindset has helped us thrive despite the odds, making Kenyans some of the most inventive and resourceful people on the planet. From jua kali (informal sector) mechanics who can fix your car with nothing but a wire hanger and some chewing gum, to students who use old plastic bottles to create solar lamps for studying at night, Kenya's innovation culture is alive and well.

But here's the kicker—while Kenya's people are naturally innovative, our national systems haven't always kept up. For too long, creativity and problem-solving were seen as the domain of "side hustles," while industries, education, and even government offices stuck to more rigid, traditional ways of doing things. Well, that's about to change. With the world moving at breakneck speed, and Kenya eager to keep up with global trends, it's time we embrace innovation not just as a buzzword, but as a national ethos.

So, let's strap in and take a deep dive into the sensational, hilarious, and often surprising world of fostering a culture of innovation in Kenya. Whether we're talking about rethinking how we teach math, developing new apps that let you avoid Nairobi traffic (if that's even possible), or inventing a way to deliver groceries via boda boda drones, this chapter is about creating a national mindset where creativity, problem-solving, and a healthy appetite for risk-taking are front and center.

Jua Kali Mentality: Innovating Without a User Manual

Let's start with the heart and soul of Kenyan innovation: the *jua kali* sector. For those unfamiliar, *jua kali* is Swahili for "hot sun," and it refers to the informal sector where entrepreneurs, mechanics, artisans, and general problem-solvers operate under the literal and metaphorical "hot sun," usually without formal training, high-tech tools, or any guarantee that whatever they're fixing will actually work. And yet, somehow, it usually does.

The *jua kali* mentality is a perfect example of innovation without limitations. In the *jua kali* world, you don't wait for a solution to fall into your lap—you create it. If your car's bumper is falling off, don't worry, some guy in a backstreet in Kariobangi has already figured out how to weld it back together using a blowtorch he rigged himself. Got a phone that's not charging? The repair guy at the market has probably fixed that problem 500 times today and will get it done faster than you can Google "nearest authorized service center."

This kind of creativity is embedded in the Kenyan spirit. It's not just about fixing things—it's about a mindset that says, "there's always a way, no matter how unconventional." While *jua kali* may sound scrappy and makeshift, the ingenuity displayed in this sector is astounding. From carpentry and metalwork to agriculture and technology, the *jua kali* sector represents a culture of innovation that thrives on resourcefulness and problem-solving. Imagine what we could achieve if this mentality was encouraged and celebrated across all sectors—especially in education, industry, and government.

Education: From "Cramming" to "Creating"

Now, let's talk about where innovation should start: the education system. For too long, Kenya's education system has been built around the idea that learning is about memorizing facts, passing exams, and getting a certificate to wave in the faces of potential employers. Don't get me wrong—there's a place for academic rigor, but if your schooling experience was anything like mine, you probably spent years learning about photosynthesis without ever understanding how that knowledge could help solve real-world problems.

The thing is, Kenya's education system has traditionally placed more emphasis on passing exams than on cultivating creativity. It's like trying to train chefs by making them memorize recipes without ever letting them into a kitchen. But in a world where automation, technology, and global competition are reshaping industries, memorizing isn't enough—we need innovators, creators, and problem-solvers. We need a system where kids can invent, experiment, and fail without fear of punishment (except maybe for setting something on fire in the chemistry lab). One exciting development is the

Competency-Based Curriculum (CBC), which aims to shift the focus from rote learning to real-world skills and problem-solving. Instead of just memorizing facts, students are encouraged to think critically, collaborate, and create. The CBC has sparked many debates—some parents love it, others would rather go back to the old system where "revision books" were the holy grail of academic success. But whatever your stance, it's clear that the future of education in Kenya has to move toward fostering innovation.

Take tech innovation hubs like **Africa Code Week**, which teach coding skills to young students in rural areas. Imagine a class of kids in a remote part of Turkana, where access to electricity is still a challenge, learning how to write code that powers mobile apps. It's not just about teaching tech—it's about planting the seeds of creativity, showing young Kenyans that they can be more than just consumers of technology. They can be creators.

And let's not forget the importance of introducing entrepreneurship in education. The next generation of Kenyan students shouldn't just be focused on getting jobs—they should be thinking about creating jobs. Schools and universities should be incubators for innovative thinking, where students learn how to turn their ideas into startups and solve real-world problems. After all, today's young Kenyan sitting in a classroom could be tomorrow's Elon Musk—except with better dancing skills at weddings.

Innovation in Industry: From Silicon Savannah to Solar-Powered Shambas

When we talk about innovation in Kenya, it's hard not to mention the rise of **Silicon Savannah**, Kenya's burgeoning tech scene. Nairobi has become the epicenter of tech innovation in Africa, home to some of the most exciting startups and disruptive technologies on the continent. Companies like **Safaricom** revolutionized mobile banking with M-Pesa, showing the world that innovation can thrive in Kenya, even when the rest of the world was still figuring out how to send a text message.

But it's not just about tech hubs and mobile apps—Kenya's innovation potential spans all industries. Take agriculture, for example. Agriculture is still the backbone of Kenya's economy, and farmers are increasingly embracing innovation to improve yields, combat climate change, and make farming more sustainable. From solar-powered irrigation systems to apps that provide real-time market prices for produce, Kenyan farmers are proving that you can combine tradition with technology to solve problems.

A fantastic (and slightly hilarious) example of this is the rise of **"agripreneurs."** These are young, tech-savvy farmers who have traded in their office jobs for shambas, using drones to monitor crops and blockchain technology to trace produce from farm to table. There's something delightfully absurd about the image of a farmer in a Maasai shuka checking his crop data on an iPhone, but that's the future of Kenyan agriculture—a blend of tech and tradition, where even the cows are probably getting fitted with GPS trackers.

Of course, with innovation comes the need for risk-taking. And in Kenya, taking risks in business can feel a bit like trying to cross Moi Avenue during rush hour—you're either going to make it to the other side unscathed, or you'll be calling your insurance agent. But Kenya's entrepreneurs have always had an appetite for risk, whether it's starting a side hustle or launching a new product in a crowded market. The key is creating an environment where failure isn't the end of the road—it's part of the journey. If there's one thing Kenya's young innovators understand, it's that failure is often the best teacher.

Government Innovation: Yes, You Read That Right

Now, let's address the elephant in the room—government. When you think of innovation, the government may not be the first thing that comes to mind. In fact, many Kenyans would argue that getting government offices to innovate is like trying to teach a fish how to ride a bicycle. But here's the thing: if Kenya is going to foster a culture of innovation, the government has to be part of the solution, not the problem.

The good news? The government has already started dipping its toes into the world of innovation, especially with initiatives like the **Huduma Centers**, which provide citizens with one-stop access to government services. Instead of navigating endless queues and piles of paperwork, Kenyans can now access critical services like ID registration, business permits, and NHIF payments under one roof. It's not exactly groundbreaking, but considering where we started, it's a pretty big deal. Plus, Huduma Centers have given us the delightful experience of seeing normally stuffy bureaucrats trying to explain mobile money to elderly wananchi (citizens) with mixed results.

Another promising development is the government's push for **digitization**. The goal is to move more services online, reducing the need for in-person visits to government offices and improving efficiency. If you've ever had to renew a passport at Nyayo House, you know that this is the kind of innovation that can literally save lives (or at least a lot of time and frustration).

But while the government's innovation efforts are laudable, there's still plenty of room for improvement. The private sector has long led the charge in technological and social innovation, and the government needs to adopt the same spirit of risk-taking, creativity, and flexibility. Imagine a world where government departments used data analytics to predict traffic patterns, where politicians held virtual town halls on YouTube, or where boda bodas were fitted with GPS trackers that automatically issued tickets for reckless driving. Is it a stretch? Maybe. But we've already got boda boda ambulances, so anything is possible.

Risk-Taking: The Innovation Playground
At the heart of innovation is risk-taking, and if there's one thing Kenya's entrepreneurs, farmers, students, and government officials need to embrace, it's the idea that failure isn't fatal. Innovation requires boldness—whether it's launching a new product, experimenting with an unconventional business model, or challenging the status quo in industries that haven't changed in decades.
In Kenya, the entrepreneurial spirit is already strong. From roadside hawkers to startup founders, Kenyans know how to hustle. But we need to take it a step further. To foster a true culture of innovation, we must create an environment where risk-taking is encouraged, failure is seen as part of the process, and success is measured not just by profits but by impact.

Think about the world's greatest innovators—Steve Jobs, Elon Musk, Oprah Winfrey—each of them failed spectacularly at some point in their careers. But they kept going because they knew that failure is simply a stepping stone to success. Kenya's innovators need the same mindset, coupled with support from educational institutions, government policies, and industry leaders.

Conclusion: A Nation of Innovators, Dreamers, and Problem-Solvers

Kenya is a nation of innovators, dreamers, and problem-solvers. Whether it's the *jua kali* mechanic fixing your car with a wire hanger, or the university student coding the next big app, the spirit of innovation is alive and well. But to truly unlock Kenya's potential, we need to foster a national culture that embraces creativity, problem-solving, and risk-taking across all sectors.

From education to industry to government, it's time to move away from rigid structures and outdated ways of thinking. We need to cultivate environments where students can experiment, entrepreneurs can take risks, and government offices can adapt to the changing needs of the public. It's not just about keeping up with global trends— it's about setting our own.

So here's to Kenya—the land of bold ideas, creative solutions, and people who know that there's always a way forward, no matter the challenge. We may not have all the answers yet, but with a little bit of innovation, a lot of hustle, and maybe a few well-placed prayers, there's no limit to what we can achieve.

KEYPOINTS AND SUMMARY

Civic Engagement's Importance: Active citizen involvement is the key to a functional and transparent government.

Accountability: Citizens must hold government leaders accountable continuously, not just during elections.

Transparency, Participation, Responsibility: These are essential principles to combat corruption, improve governance, and create lasting change.

Examples of Civic Action: Movements like #MyDressMyChoice, Unga Revolution, and #StopTheseThieves show the impact of collective action.

Civic Action Improves Public Services: When citizens unite, they influence better services and governance.

Call to Action: Civic engagement empowers individuals to build a better, accountable nation.

Media's Role: Media in Kenya shapes national identity, holds leaders accountable, and fosters public discourse.

Evolution of Media: From government-controlled broadcasts in the 1980s to today's diverse media landscape, including social media and #KOT (Kenyans on Twitter).

Accountability: Media, especially investigative journalism, exposes scandals and corruption.

Digital Media's Power: Social media empowers citizens to engage in political and social issues, but also brings challenges like fake news.

Media Literacy: Critical in combating misinformation and ensuring a well-informed society.

Shaping National Identity: Media reflects Kenya's culture, values, and democratic journey.

Kenya's Innovation Culture: Embraces "mwanaume ni kujaribu" (life is about trying), fostering a spirit of creativity and problem-solving, especially in the informal "jua kali" sector.

Education Reform: The Competency-Based Curriculum (CBC) promotes critical thinking, real-world skills, and innovation over rote learning.

Tech and Industry: Silicon Savannah and innovative agriculture showcase Kenya's tech potential, blending tradition with technology.

Government's Role: Efforts like Huduma Centers and digitization show government strides in innovation, though more is needed.

Risk-Taking: Encouraging boldness and risk-taking is key to unlocking Kenya's full innovation potential.

Conclusion

A Call to Action – Together, We Can Build a Better Kenya

As we come to the end of this book, it's time to talk about the most important part: **you**. Yes, you—the reader, the citizen, the dreamer, the person who wants to see Kenya grow, prosper, and become the shining beacon of hope it was always meant to be. Because here's the thing: no matter how many chapters we write, how many plans we propose, or how many ideas we generate, none of it matters without action. And that action? It starts with each one of us. So let's roll up our sleeves and talk about how we can build a better Kenya, one step at a time.

1. Reaffirm the Vision for a New Kenya

Before we dive into what needs to be done, let's revisit why we're doing it. The vision we laid out at the beginning of this journey was bold: a **Kenya of integrity, unity, innovation, and sustainable development**. It's a vision where corruption doesn't drain our resources, where tribalism doesn't divide us, where every citizen—regardless of background—has a seat at the table. It's a vision where innovation thrives, where new ideas are nurtured, and where entrepreneurship drives economic growth. And it's a vision where we protect our environment for future generations, ensuring that Kenya remains not only a beautiful place to live but a sustainable one.

The hope for this new Kenya is grounded in **transparency**, **inclusivity**, and **national pride**. We want a country where leaders serve the people, not themselves; where businesses flourish because they innovate, not because they cut corners; and where every Kenyan—whether living in the city or in the village—feels proud to call this place home. We're not just talking about development for the sake of it. We're talking about a Kenya where **every citizen thrives**. So as we move forward, let's keep this vision in mind.

2. Highlight the Collective Responsibility

Here's the truth that we can't ignore: building a better Kenya is a **collective responsibility**. It's not the job of politicians alone, nor is it something that can be left to NGOs or big businesses. It requires **every single one of us** to step up and do our part. Whether you're a government official, a leader in the private sector, a community activist, or an everyday Kenyan just trying to get by, you have a role to play.

Let's talk about **active citizenship**. Being a good citizen is more than just paying taxes and showing up on election day (though both are essential!). It's about engaging with the issues that affect your community, holding leaders accountable, and standing up for what's right. It's about participating in civic duty—whether that means voting, volunteering, or simply speaking out when you see something that's wrong. As citizens, we need to understand that **change begins at the individual level**.

For example, imagine if every Kenyan refused to pay or accept a bribe. What kind of country would we live in? Corruption would crumble. Imagine if every community came together to tackle local problems, whether that's organizing trash clean-ups, mentoring youth, or planting trees to combat climate change. These are the kinds of **small, individual actions** that, when multiplied by millions of Kenyans, can create a tidal wave of positive change.

3. Call for Immediate and Long-Term Actions

So what can we do? Let's break it down into **immediate actions** you can take today, and **long-term commitments** that will shape the Kenya of tomorrow.

Immediate Actions:

- **Fight corruption** by refusing to engage in or tolerate corrupt practices. It starts small—report that traffic officer asking for a bribe, refuse to grease the palm of a government official. Integrity starts with each one of us.

- **Volunteer in community-driven projects**. There are thousands of grassroots initiatives across Kenya that are making a difference. Whether it's tutoring young students, building wells, or advocating for women's rights, there's a space for you to contribute.

- **Support local entrepreneurs and sustainable businesses**. Kenya's economy is built on the spirit of entrepreneurship. By supporting local businesses, you're helping to create jobs, encourage innovation, and build a stronger economy. Look for businesses that prioritize sustainability, because they're the ones ensuring we don't deplete our resources for future generations.

- **Participate in civic discussions and policymaking processes**. Whether it's attending a town hall meeting, engaging in a Twitter debate, or joining a local advocacy group, make your voice heard. Democracy isn't just about casting a ballot—it's about shaping the policies that affect your life.

Long-Term Solutions:

- **Invest in education**. As a nation, we need to prioritize education—not just by sending kids to school, but by ensuring that our education system teaches critical thinking, creativity, and problem-solving. This is how we create the next generation of leaders and innovators who will take Kenya to new heights.

- **Environmental stewardship**. Climate change is real, and its effects are already being felt in Kenya. From droughts to floods, we need to get serious about protecting our environment. Plant trees, reduce waste, and support initiatives that promote sustainable farming and clean energy.

- **Intergenerational leadership development**. Let's not forget about the future. We need to invest in **youth leadership** and mentorship programs that empower the next generation of Kenyans to step into leadership roles. It's not just about preparing future leaders—it's about giving them the tools they need to lead with integrity and innovation.

A Nation Built on Action, Not Just Words

If you've made it this far, you're probably fired up about all the potential Kenya has, and you're ready to jump in and do your part. But here's the thing: **words alone won't build a better Kenya**. We've talked about what needs to change, we've laid out the vision, and we've highlighted the challenges and opportunities. Now, it's time to act. This book is meant to inspire, but more importantly, it's meant to challenge you to take these ideas and **turn them into reality**.

We can't afford to sit back and wait for someone else to make the change. The responsibility is ours—yours and mine. It's time to move from **talking about the Kenya we deserve** to actually building it. We need to work together, push past the obstacles, and create a country that thrives on

integrity, **innovation**, and **unity**. A Kenya where we don't just survive—we **flourish**.

A Final Thought: The Kenya We Will Leave Behind
As we look ahead to the future, it's worth asking ourselves one final question: **What kind of Kenya do we want to leave behind for future generations?** Will it be a country where corruption, division, and inequality continue to hold us back? Or will it be a Kenya where integrity, unity, and innovation drive us forward into a brighter, more prosperous future?
The answer is in our hands. We have the power to create a **Kenya we can all be proud of**, but it's going to take hard work, dedication, and a relentless commitment to the values we hold dear. So, let's not wait for tomorrow. **Let's start today.**

Together, we can build a better Kenya—one where every citizen plays their part, one where every child has the opportunity to dream big, and one where our national pride isn't just something we talk about, but something we live every day.

And with that, let's get to work. **Kenya is calling, and it's time to answer.**

www.ingramcontent.com/pod-product-compliance
Lightning Source LLC
Chambersburg PA
CBHW061333250726
48657CB00004B/1146